TEACHING ENGLISH

How to Teach English as a Second Language (ESL)

By Mark Beales

Published by Dram Publishing

Copyright: 2021 Mark Beales

All Rights Reserved.

ISBN: 978-0-9572823-8-4

Contents

Chapter 1: Why teach?

Chapter 2: What does it take?

Chapter 3: Types of Teachers

Chapter 4: Types of students

Chapter 5: Teaching Theory

Chapter 6: Enter the classroom

Chapter 7: Discipline

Chapter 8: How to make it interesting

Chapter 9: Grammar - the basics

Chapter 10: The Four Skills

Chapter 11: Culture Clash

Chapter 12: Assessments

Chapter 13: Where to teach?

Chapter 14: Websites and resources

Chapter 15: Glossary of acronyms and terms

Chapter 16: Reference Books

About the Author

CHAPTER 1: WHY TEACH?

So you think you can teach...

When it comes to picking your dream job, some options leap out at you. Wine taster, travel writer, movie critic: who wouldn't fancy any of those? Teaching, on the other hand, is a more maligned profession.

Days spent trying to control unruly pseudo-anarchists and nights spent marking their indecipherable work is the usual image. However, what if teaching involved getting to live abroad, experiencing new cultures and having ten weeks holiday a year to explore your new surroundings?

The idea of being able to teach by the beach is increasingly popular; to spread the delights of the English language to a few dozen students who eagerly lap up every clause and conjunction before you head off to your hammock to sip an icy beer as the sun dips under the horizon.

OK, so reality may not always be as idyllic, but teaching English as a Second Language (ESL) can be an incredibly rewarding experience. Sorry about the acronym so early on but, if you're going to teach, you'll have to get used to it.

This book is designed to offer practical insights into exactly what steps you need to take to land a teaching job. It will also tell you how to teach and reveal some of the secrets and tips to surviving in a country where the culture may be alien.

We won't just show you the difference between an adverb and an adjective; you'll also learn some essential practical advice, such as why you should never teach the word 'judo' to Thai teenage boys.

My experience of teaching includes basic government establishments, private colleges and international schools. I've taught students who could barely write their name in English through to those who studied Shakespeare and Chaucer. When dealing with office politics I've learned to bite my tongue so hard there's now an indelible impression inside my mouth, but on the other hand I've had a letter from Queen Elizabeth II (well, her hand maiden) praising my students. Teaching ESL is many things, but it's never dull.

Every day is different and brings its own challenges and rewards. Sometimes it's the little things that stay with you. One of my favourite moments came during an examination. As I walked around to check on students, a boy put his hand up. I walked over and the boy declared: "Sir, I no cheat."

A little confused as the exam had only started, I said: "Congratulations, son."

He frowned, and then repeated: "No, no, Mr Mark, I don't cheat."

"Yes, that's right. 'I don't cheat', is better than 'I no cheat'. I understand, well done."

Exasperated at my lack of comprehension, he finally grabbed his friend's question paper and yelled: "No, I no have sheet, I need a sheet."

Why learn English?

English isn't the most widely-spoken language on the planet. That honour goes to Chinese. However, while knowing Chinese is advantageous if you're in China, it's of limited use anywhere else.

English is simply the global language. It's the language of aviation, shipping, international business and, largely, the internet. It also happens to be a language that befuddles, bemuses and bamboozles even native speakers with its complexities and nuances. It's a language that is so varied that while someone from Australia may have a vastly different vocabulary and accent from someone in California or Barbados, they can still all get along.

The reasons for its complexities can be found in the history books (invading Danes, Romans and French all left parts of their languages in Britain). The reasons for its global influence begin with the slave trade. When the British began using slaves from Africa, they separated them from those with whom they shared a mother tongue to ensure the only common language was English. Britain's colonial empire also ensured the language spread to Australia, India and the Caribbean.

More recently, America's economic dominance has ensured that English has flourished: Is there anywhere left in the world where a 'Big Mac' is unknown? It may be a hugely useful language to have, but not everyone is impressed by its seeming ability to conquer all. The French get very uptight about English, so much so that in 1996 erstwhile President Jacques Chirac stormed out of an EU meeting in a row over the lingua franca. Mr Chirac was annoyed by his countryman Ernest-Antoine Seilliere, who changed to English during his speech, as he called it 'the language of business'.

In Africa, many authors write in English in order to reach a wider audience. Chinua Achebe is perhaps the best-known African writer thanks to 'Things Fall Apart', but many of his contemporaries criticised him for writing in the tongue of the coloniser and oppressor. Achebe argued that the only way to change ill-conceived notions over pre-colonial history was to write in English.

Clearly, teachers should not promote the idea that English is somehow 'better' than their students' native tongues; however in most countries it usually gives you an edge, and that is why so many want to learn it. Demand for learning English has never been as high (there are now more Chinese learning English than there are native English speakers) so if you do choose to teach, you'll never have to look too hard for work. Many who planned to teach only for a year or two during a career gap find that teaching soon becomes their new career – and a gateway to living and working in many parts of the world.

CHAPTER 2: WHAT DOES IT TAKE?

What do I need?

Having decided that you want to teach, the next step is to see whether schools may actually want you. Most countries have set rules about who they want teaching their students. Typically, if you have a degree in any subject and of any grade, then you're half way there. If you happen to have a degree in education, congratulations, you've just hit the jackpot.

Assuming you do have a degree, the next step is to get a TEFL (Teaching English as a Foreign Language) Certificate. These come in all shapes, sizes and colours. Your average school isn't going to fret over what kind you have, but it is worth investing in a reputable course as the knowledge gained will be invaluable once you enter the classroom.

It is possible to do courses in your home country or abroad. Courses in the country you're planning to make your base are a good choice as you can start to understand the culture while getting qualified, and have free time to explore your new surroundings. Most courses run for 3-4 weeks and give you a certificate at the end with the door-opening acronym TEFL emblazoned on it.

Most courses are reputable, but be wary of those who pledge to find you a job placement as soon as the course is over, then only hand over the certificate once you've completed several months with your new employer. Chances are the agency has a deal with the school that gives them a cut of your salary. After four months you may well be out of work as the next new teacher is being lined up to take your place. The school may not be getting seasoned teachers, but then it isn't having to spend time recruiting either.

Most agencies are, however, reputable and many will help you find work without any catches, but it's wise to be wary and ask questions first. Course costs are broadly similar and will set you back around $500-$600. At the top end the Certificate in English Language Teaching to Adults (CELTA) is the Manchester United of TEFL certificates, while distance learning ones are considered to be the Doncaster Rovers. Distance learning courses offer a good insight into teaching theory and how to prepare lessons, but you don't get to actually teach in front of anyone. The CELTA costs around $1500 and while, as its name suggests, it is geared towards teaching adults, most schools will gladly accept that you know what you're doing if you wave one under their noses.

Having a degree is a legal requirement to teach in most schools, but if you don't have one there is still good money to be made teaching Business English to adults. Some folk actually prefer this, as there is far less paperwork and the students are generally more motivated (they're probably paying to see you, after all). There is also demand for online tutors, who can work from anywhere in the world and make reasonable money, if they put the hours in. Every country has slightly different rules too, so be flexible and realistic.

If you didn't go to university, don't pretend that you did. You may be able to bluff your way through an interview and produce a certificate upon which the ink has just dried; you may also be able to work as a teacher as many places don't bother to check qualifications or references. However all it takes is one phone call to immigration and you won't just lose your job, you could lose your freedom. Several teachers have been jailed for falsely claiming to have degrees. As yet, no-one has ever been jailed for saying they don't have one.

It's not worth trying to bypass the rules and regulations. The same goes for so-called 'Life Degrees' that you can pick up online. They are utterly worthless and if a school falls for it then you should question whether you want to work for a place that gives so little thought about who they want to teach their students. One slight addendum: rules often change and so it's worth looking at online forums for the latest requirements, but if you have a TEFL certificate, you'll be in prime position.

Visas and Work Permits

Living in a country, as opposed to holidaying in one, means you may need to think about visas and work permits. For teachers this should be relatively simple, as schools tend to sort out such things.

Visas are straightforward as long as you read the small print and provide what officers are looking for, even if it is occasionally a little 'extra' to make things go smoothly.

While the visa allows you to remain in a country beyond the normal tourist limits, you may also need a work permit to actually work. Some schools overlook the work permit as they consider their job done once the visa arrives however it is worth pushing for the permit as well.

What will my school be like?

Class sizes can range from six to 60. Accordingly, so do standards. In many countries, there are three strata of schools. At the bottom of the rung are government schools. These typically only employ a handful of foreigners (as you're an expensive luxury).

Class sizes in government schools can be enormous; 50 in a class is not exceptional. Fees are relatively cheap, and so this is where most students are sent. A foreign teacher here would tend to get a salary that is equivalent to, or better than, the average wage, plus a good amount of holiday. Make sure it's paid holiday before you sign up.

The second tier is private colleges, where class sizes could be between 25 and 40 students. Middle class families tend to choose these colleges as much for networking reasons as academic ones. It's never a bad thing when your classmate's father builds houses for a living and you happen to supply imported furniture that would look splendid inside such homes.

Many of these mid-tier schools run English Programmes, where for an extra fee your child will meet foreign teachers on a regular basis. Private schools employ more foreign teachers so you can expect more folk to hang out with. Perks may include free health insurance, an end-of-contract bonus and, if you're fortunate, a flight bonus.

At the highest echelon are the international schools. There are relatively few of these, and most of them will probably be based around the capital city or industrial centres (as that's where foreign parents will be working). Internationals are nearly always based on the British, American or Australian curricula, and employ career teachers. Class sizes can be tiny and anything over 20 to a class is considered cramped. UK-based teachers will hold a Post-Graduate Certificate of Education (PGCE), which for many is the Holy Grail of teaching.

Many foreigners start by teaching ESL and then decide to make more of a commitment and gain the PGCE. The prime reason for this is hard cash. Teach in an international school and you can triple your ESL salary, along with all the trimmings. If you have children they will normally get free schooling, worth tens of thousands of dollars a year.

Students at international schools are a different breed. Not only will most speak English fluently, they will also tend to be far more independent, organised and motivated than pupils from local schools. ESL teachers can still find work here, as new students who don't yet possess adequate English skills will be given intensive language lessons to get them up to speed. Salaries for ESL teachers at international schools are better than regular ESL teachers but generally fall short of mainstream teachers' wages. Paying so much means schools can be picky and you'll need three years' experience plus the qualifications - or happen to be in the right place at the right time - to land a gig in one.

Another option is to teach Business English. Large multinational companies need to train Thai staff to deal with international customers, so demand for teachers is always high. Many ESL teachers supplement their salaries with this kind of work, which pays at least $15 an hour. Some prefer Business English as they teach adults who are more motivated than students, and are often just as much fun.

Look for industrial estates and/or language schools nearby. Make friends with either of these and you'll soon find extra work.

Universities will also take on ESL teachers who have taught for a couple of years. Paradoxically, the level of university English in many developing countries often isn't any different from in high schools. Wages aren't much different either, unless you make your way to the more elite institutions. Despite being the highest level of education a country can offer, some universities are not too fussy when it comes to quality. That could be why one writing course we heard of featured a tutor who couldn't actually spell the word 'review' or 'brief'. Or, best of all, 'writing'.

How do I get a job?

By far the most common way to find work is via the internet. Google 'ESL' plus the name of your chosen country and a bevy of sites should pop up, each with plenty of advertisements for vacancies.

Read the adverts carefully and only apply if you are suitable. If the job wants native speakers only then that's code for no Filipinos, if they ask for someone under 50 they mean it, and if they want a one-eyed New Yorker with a limp then get over it, there are plenty more jobs around.

Make sure you have a CV that is well-written, covers the essentials and is grammatically accurate (you'd be amazed how many English teachers can't master this last part). If you're starting out, find out when schools in your country start their new academic year and aim to apply then. If you go job-hunting just after a term has already started, your chances dip dramatically.

Of course, if you have your heart set on a particular school, then mail them directly. Don't turn up unannounced as such a show of spontaneity won't be appreciated.

It's worth being aware that some schools are pretty fussy about what they are looking for. Glance at any jobs section of a newspaper and you'll notice that such pedantry is common. Some only want females, some only want females under 30, and some want females under 30 who are 'attractive'. The kind of adverts that would see you sued back home are regular features in some parts. Employers have the upper hand and aren't afraid to say what they want: we know of one school that even bans men with facial hair. They once employed a Sikh chap, assuming they could ask him nicely if he could go for a haircut and shave, before discovering that wasn't really an option from someone of that faith.

Skin colour is, unfortunately, also an issue. Asian countries have a pecking order when it comes to colour. It's no defence but it does seem to be based more around actual skin colour rather than ethnic groups. Some nations simply see dark skin as less attractive than white skin, and aren't shy about saying so. One reason is the power of marketing. In Thailand, television presenters have vanilla-white tones while comedy shows regularly 'black-up' actors, and then proceed to poke fun at them. During the advertising breaks you can hear about how by simply applying some whitening lotion to your face you'll find true love and eternal joy. A company for a skin-whitening lotion once placed an advert saying 'reserved for whites only' on the Bangkok sky train before more worldly-wise folk pointed out its apartheid connotations and demanded its removal. Perhaps the best example of how Thai sensitivities differ from those in the West can be found on a tube of toothpaste. A toothpaste company once inexplicably decided to call its product 'Darkie'. Given that this is the one product where whiteness actually is a key component, it did seem a tad incongruous. As if 'Darkie' weren't bad enough, the toothpaste's logo was the face of a black and white minstrel. Only in the past few years has the concept of race relations entered the local psyche, and now it's been renamed 'Darlie' – though the minstrel logo remains.

Another theory for the preference for white skin is that black skin is associated with upcountry farmers who have to toil out in the fields every day. Far more preferable to be educated and rich, and get to work in air-conditioned offices where you can avoid going dark.

The thinking is clearly misguided, but there usually isn't much malice involved; some places just haven't got round to focusing on race relations. None of which helps much if you aren't Caucasian and looking for work.

Some schools are pickier than others; a few I heard of turned away black candidates at the gate – not letting them even enter the premises. Such extreme responses are rare, and a native speaking teacher with a degree and TEFL will eventually still find work, whatever their race.

How do I get past the interview?

Interviews for ESL jobs work in a similar way to any other interview. Observe the obvious – be punctual, be presentable and be pleasant.

Remember that this is your chance to sell yourself and explain just how badly the school needs someone like you. Stick to the essentials; the school probably doesn't want to hear about you landed in their nation after your ex-wife walked out and you lost your job, which is the dead-end alley some interviews tend to stumble down.

Classic, if slightly staid, interview questions include:

'Tell me about your greatest strengths and weaknesses as a teacher'.

'How would you handle class discipline?'

'You have a 50 minute class on the Present Continuous Tense, how would you plan it?'

'What did you think of your TEFL course?'

'Which areas do you feel you need to develop?'

Towards the end of the interview, you'll probably be asked if you have any questions. Prepare a few in advance, even if you know everything you need to. The interview is as much for you to decide if you want to work at this school as it is for the school to see if it wants you, so you should naturally have some queries. Ask about the classroom facilities, find out about extra-curricular activities, and see what course books they use. Do not ask about pay, perks or holidays at this point as it gives the wrong impression.

The interview is also the time where you can get to size up your potential employer. Think about what you expect from your school (air-conditioning, projectors and a range of resources are a good place to start). If you don't like what you see, then don't take it.

Sometimes, the interviewer can be a good clue about the state of the school. In one interview I helped conduct, the other guy had a nasty habit of interjecting with comments when he really didn't need to. He once decided to ask a nervous-looking, middle-aged applicant about his personal background.

'Well, I was married for 10 years, got divorced, and fancied a move abroad. I came on holiday here last year and met a nice young lady so decided to move out. I just got here on Tuesday,' the applicant said

'Ahh, fresh meat,' the interviewer smirked.

We didn't hear from the guy again. Not all interviewers are as obnoxious as this one, but it does show the importance of making a good first impression and remembering which details to leave out. One final point, have a basic demo lesson up your sleeve, just in case.

If you are offered the job then congratulations, you're about to enter the wonderful world of ESL. The next step is to get used to your new school and most importantly, your new colleagues.

CHAPTER 3: TYPES OF TEACHERS

What makes a good teacher?

Think back to your favourite teacher at school. What was it that made him or her stand out? Chances are if you ask 10 people this, they'd come up with broadly similar qualities.

Have a look at these attributes and decide which you'd put near the top of your list, and which are less important.

- Kind and patient
- Fun
- Good at motivating students
- Good knowledge of the subject
- Knows how to get the best out of every student
- Explains things clearly

The first three items above deal with personality, while the last three are more about professional skills. There isn't one finite answer for how to create the perfect teacher, but if there were, it would probably include most of the above.

As well as being a teacher, that is, standing up and explaining stuff, you will also take on several other roles in your classroom, depending on what you want students to do.

These extra roles could be:

The boss (the sage on the stage) – a traditional role where you tell students what they are going to do. For this, the teacher needs a strong personality and the ability to deliver clear, concise, instructions.

The facilitator (the guide on the side) – setting things up then taking a back seat and letting students get on with a task. It can be tempting to jump straight in when there's a problem but often it's better to let students work things out.

The guide – teachers often need to give examples before letting students practise something. You may be the only English voice they hear all day, so be clear and correct.

The judge – once students have completed a task, they'll want to know how they've done. It's best to offer feedback at the end of a task, especially if that task involves speaking. Always find something positive to say, even if it was a disaster. Covering a book with red ink as you correct work can be disheartening, so you don't need to always point out every mistake. Better to focus on the same mistake that's made several times. Some teachers don't even use red ink as they feel it's too aggressive. As long as the colour is different from that of the student's work, it doesn't really matter what you use.

The helper – students will get stuck. When this happens, the teacher's role is to step in and prod the student in the right direction, without completely taking over. You can lead a student towards the answer, but always try and make sure they are the ones that actually say it.

It Takes All Sorts

Think about the job you do now. There's a good chance that the people in your office aren't all that different from yourself (even if you don't like to admit it).

If you're in PR then you're probably in a room full of outgoing, creative and media-savvy. If you're a journalist your colleagues may have a dry sense of humour, a sense of justice and neat turn of phrase. If you're a car mechanic you probably like football, a laugh and Formula 1. OK, we're perilously close to cliché here, but you get the point. Similar jobs tend to attract similar people.

This theory goes out the window when it comes to ESL. People become ESL teachers for all kinds of reasons. Nowhere else will you find such a mélange of backgrounds, attitudes and beliefs, which is what makes the ESL staffroom like no other you'll ever work in.

People teach English for all kinds of reasons but most seem to fit into one of the following categories:

1. **The backpacker:** Straight out of uni on a gap year, they plan to fit in a bit of teaching in between weekend breaks to the islands and bars. Those that focus on teaching can make great ESL teachers as they're young, enthusiastic and can relate to students – after all, they were one a few months ago. Their one drawback is that as they are young, some students don't see them as adult figures and so they need to work harder to gain respect.

2. **The divorcee:** The idea of living abroad and starting again attracts many newly-single, middle-aged men, and sometimes women. Given their one common denominator is the lack of a wedding ring, this group can vary wildly in terms of quality.

3. **The change-of-scene teacher:** That two-week break last summer was so memorable they simply couldn't stay away. So following a TEFL course they're now ready for anything.

During my career I've witnessed an incredible array of characters, some of whom will remain friends for life, while others I'd cross the street to avoid. Living abroad can be a lonely experience too, so you tend to socialize with people you wouldn't normally hang out with, which lets you experience the full spectrum of human behavior.

Here are some of the most memorable teachers.

The Good, the Bad and the Unlucky

The Good

There's an old Chinese proverb that says 'A teacher opens the door. You have to walk through by yourself'. Some teachers seem to have a natural gift for opening the door and persuading students that what's on the other side is worth pursuing.

A few teachers just make that extra effort to go beyond what's in the book. They engage, they enthuse and energise students simply by knowing what they are talking about.

There are times when being a teacher feels like you're a Sesame Street presenter. Sticky-back plastic, coloured paper and 3-D posters suddenly become the norm. Some teachers spend an hour or more creating artwork for their classroom and cutting out fancy fonts to highlight students' work on a regular basis.

Other teachers have such a presence that you can't help but listen, whatever the subject. It isn't always the best-qualified or most-experienced teachers that get the greatest results; some have simply embarked on a new career and want to make the most of it. Teaching is incredibly rewarding when it goes well, and whether it goes well often depends on a teacher's approach to their job.

The Bad

There's another adage that says: 'The secret of teaching is to appear to have known all your life what you learned this afternoon.'

Teachers who take this approach are often the ones who end up with the noisiest classes and students who don't understand, and so subsequently don't care.

They also happen to provide the best anecdotes. One of the first teachers I encountered was a large American who had a clear aversion to living everywhere other than America. He'd taught in South Korea and Europe, and hated both, and so was hoping to find Thailand more to his liking. On his first day he complained that it was too hot and it went downhill from there. He lurched between mood swings like a man who had won the lottery and been given two days to live.

During my first months at school Jason and I shared the same apartment block. I had a car and so gave him lifts into work every morning. Every morning he would come down late and then on the way to work roll down my window and launch a huge, and noisy, gob of phlegm out of my car window.

On a Monday morning his mood depended on whether he'd spent the weekend in Bangkok smoking weed. If he had, all would be well with the world and the smell of tuk-tuk fumes would seem like the scent of freshly-cut daisies. If he hadn't, then Thais were blood-sucking parasites who were out to get him.

Working in Asian schools means being presented with situations that often don't seem logical, but having to deal with them regardless. Jason didn't deal with anything well. At school he would swear and stomp around for no good reason.

The rainy season was particularly distressing for him. During one storm he tried to cross the road and, when a motorbike inadvertently splashed him, he delivered some of his phlegm in its direction. During another rainy day a tuk-tuk driver refused to give him a lift into work. By the time a sodden Jason reached the office he spent the first five minutes cursing all tuk-tuk drivers. He then placed his wet shoes up on his desk to let them dry, and put his bare feet the desk, soles pointing directly at the door. In Asian culture the soles of your feet are the dirtiest part of the body – physically and spiritually - and are not shown to anybody. You don't point with your feet, you don't touch people with them, you just leave them on the floor. Pointing the soles of your feet towards a door is just about the most offensive sign you could make to a Thai. It's like flicking someone the finger the second they walk into the room.

Jason tended to take out his frustrations on anyone who would listen, but once he extended this to his students. As the Christmas break approached classes were more lethargic than usual and he was keen for school to be over. In one class Jason was trying to persuade students to open their books (a task that can take 2 minutes even on a good day). One student wasn't listening. Jason called his name a couple of times and found no response. He asked another student to prod him but this also failed to provoke a reaction. Exasperated, Jason picked up the nearest object, which happened to be a miniature Christmas tree, and launched it in the student's direction. The tree hit the student plum on the forehead. A small trickle of blood started to appear.

Sensing he'd finally gone too far, Jason couldn't apologise enough, although the student didn't seem bothered. All the same, Jason took the next day off sick in case an irate parent called in. If there is a lesson to be learned from Jason, it was that living abroad isn't supposed to be like home and if you can't accept that, perhaps you'd be better off staying where you are.

Pete, on the other hand, was the most ebullient chap you're ever likely to meet. From the heart of Texas, he was a former Marine with a story for every occasion. He could talk for hours without drawing breath and was highly entertaining, even if the local female staff rarely had a clue whether he was hitting on them or laughing at them (it was usually the former).

During his first week we took him and some other new teachers to the local bank to open an account. Pete's incessant chatter soon earned him a stern stare from the matriarch-like manager.

The bank was more like a library with its hushed voices and so this talking tornado wasn't appreciated.

The manager was doing her best though and using her limited English to ask questions. Eventually she got round to Pete.

"So where you from?"

"Texas, ma'am."

"Ah, you cowboy yes?"

"Yes, ma'am, a true cowboy, yeee-har."

Unfortunately for Pete, 'eeee-har' roughly translates to the F-word in Thai. He'd shattered the silence in the bank by punching the air as he yelled 'yeeee-har', and all of a sudden the manager wasn't quite so keen to chat. She muttered something to her colleagues and handed us over to an underling.

Pete apparently had a child somewhere in the south but there didn't seem any rush towards a reunion. Instead Pete focused much of his time on finding a LBFB (little brown f*** buddy), as he put it.

When it came to schoolwork Pete taught science, and taught it rather well (he'd been in the Marines' medical corps). When it came to teaching biology, Pete hit upon the idea of bringing in four baby pigs for the students to dissect. Having found a pig market near the school he secured four live pigs for 200 baht each, and then set about trying to kill them in his small apartment.

In the staffroom the following morning he described the carnage.

'Man, that was brutal. I got hold of some ether to knock them out, but it didn't work so well. I covered one of them pigs with the ether and it passed out. Then as soon as I start dealing with the second one, the first one perks up and starts struggling.

"Eventually I had to cut its throat, but the damn thing still struggled. I should have had a giant hammer. Apartment looks like a damned George Romero movie set."

In between slaughtering pigs and offending bank staff, Pete was entertaining, though he had a remarkable knack for finding trouble. Every Monday morning he would tell us of a scrap he had got into at the weekend. This was even more remarkable given that after nearly a year in Thailand, I'd yet to notice a raised eyebrow. You have to really make an effort to rile a Thai, but once you do, you'd best stand back. Pete discovered this after talking to four girls outside a club. When their boyfriends showed up, Pete wasn't keen to admit defeat, and before long a scuffle broke out. Despite being outnumbered Pete could handle himself, and it was only when his bike toppled over on top of him that he succumbed. The resultant broken ankle meant he couldn't walk upstairs to classrooms, and the school soon decided it would be better off without him.

Some teachers weren't annoying or rude; they just weren't very good. Bob from Britain is a great example. Bob worked at a time when the powers that be were getting keen to inspect everyone's credentials. As Bob didn't have any, this was a problem. To get around any suspicion, Bob invented a glorious past with a stellar education. If he had only done some more research, he might have got away with it.

'Yes, I remember going to Grammar School when I was younger' he would say assuredly to anyone who would listen. 'Grammar Schools aren't what you'd expect though; they don't just do grammar.'

After Grammar School, it seems Bob went to a respectable university, where he gained a BA in Zoology. Given that zoology is traditionally a science-based qualification, you may well expect it to be a BSc, but minor details like this simply didn't bother Bob.

Strangely, after achieving such academic heights, he ended up working as a baggage handler at Heathrow before opting for a career in education. Bob also had a tendency to whine and moan about local people in a staffroom full of local people. He assumed they didn't understand, but they got the gist of things, and he was soon out.

Other folk are able to teach perfectly well, they just can't get along with anyone. A science teacher once fell out with a colleague with peculiar consequences. Every morning this teacher would sit in the staff room and studiously pour two Red Bulls into a bottle of Coke, so it was hardly surprising that he was highly-strung. This tension finally snapped after one petty row. I entered the staff room after one lesson and found that this teacher's desk was missing. The teacher had decamped into the adjacent library and was planning to work from there. It took a few minutes to persuade him that the library was a little too large for one teacher and he needed to move his table back.

Sex is another reason that some Westerns move to other countries. Developing countries often have a reputation for more hedonistic principles, and so holiday-makers sometimes like the place so much they decide to come and work there.

One such teacher was in his 60s and rather rotund. Not that this stopped him making weekly trips down the road to a strip of bars where he could indulge in the pleasures of the flesh. Schools will generally turn a blind eye to such behaviour, but this guy went out of his way to boast of his exploits. During one seminar we had some invited guests come to tell us about classroom management. As a warmer, they asked this chap and another to stand and run through a brief conversation.

'So, John, how are you today?'

'I'm grand, thank you.'

'And what are you going to do this weekend?'

John didn't miss a beat and replied in a booming voice: 'I'm going down the road to commit sin.'

Our stony-faced Head of Department put her head in her hands and within three months, he was out.

The Unlucky

You'll have noted that the list of bad teachers is considerably longer than that of the good ones. It isn't that there are more hopeless ESL teachers than proficient ones; it's just that the bad ones are more interesting to read about. As well as good and bad, there are simply those that fall victim to the idiosyncrasies of life in a foreign country. Sometimes you can just be in the wrong place at the wrong time.

James was a qualified football coach, and a decent teacher. When his daughter fell seriously ill, he rushed back home to England to be with her. James made a point of telling his school where he was and how long he'd be away. When his daughter started to recover, James changed his flights so he could return to work a few days earlier than planned.

Once back, he rang the Head of Department to let her know – and was told he'd been sacked and didn't need to come in on Monday.

Somewhat taken aback, James tried to ask why but the phone had gone dead. It turned out that he had told his travel plans to another foreign teacher, not the Head of Department. That might not seem a particularly heinous act, but said teacher and the Head didn't get along, so the Head felt she'd lost face by not being told directly of James' plans.

All rather silly, you might think, but it does illustrate the importance of the hierarchy in some foreign cultures. Don't assume messages will be passed on and everyone kept informed. If you want somebody to know something, tell them yourself. As well as crossing 't's and dotting 'i's, you'll also need to cover your back.

Matthew was another teacher to be caught up in such a mess. He claimed to have a degree, one of the prerequisites for teaching in Thailand. Having gained a job, he made no secret of the fact that his qualification was bogus. When another teacher fell out of favour and was sacked, he felt pretty piqued by the manner of his dismissal. So much so that he decided to make life hard for his Head of Department. The best way of doing this seemed to be to raise as many red flags as he could about his former colleagues. He e-mailed his former school, threatening to pay a visit to immigration if certain degree-less teachers weren't dismissed. Soon after, Matthew was looking for another job.

If you play things straight, you'll rarely have problems teaching. If you don't play things straight you will often get away with it, but when things do start crashing down, they tend to collapse in one almighty heap.

Wherever you end up teaching, the chances are that you are going to be alongside people you'd never normally work with, which can make the whole experience more memorable, one way or another.

CHAPTER 4: TYPES OF STUDENTS

If you think language teachers may come in a range of shapes and sizes, just wait until you witness the range of students you're going to teach.

Some students are eager, some are recalcitrant; some students are delightful, some are dire. However, the good news is that to a large extent the kind of student you get is related to the kind of teacher you are. Plan well, think how to engage with students and there's a good chance they will react positively.

Go somewhere like South Korea, and you're likely to meet students who live in a society where work and education are paramount and so they'll have their heads in their books from dawn to dusk. Head to Japan and you may be met with willing, charming students who don't want to interact for fear of making a mistake. Or land in a Thai classroom and you will need to be as much an entertainer as you will a teacher. If you make a lesson anything there, make it stimulating. The first complaint Thai students usually have is that lessons aren't 'sanuk', or fun.

Depending on where you are teaching, students' levels of English may vary wildly. At the top of the ladder are international schools, where students only study ESL until they ready to join mainstream classes. And on the bottom rung are government schools, with classes of 50-plus. Traditional teaching methodology in such environments often focuses on reading and writing, with plenty of drilling. The results are that students that can recite the formula for the Passive Future Continuous Tense, but may have few speaking and listening activities. As well as various types of schools, the various ages of students will also affect how you teach. Below is a breakdown of the basic student groups you can expect.

Young Children

Trying to find teachers to work in kindergarten can be like attempting to count the stars in a night sky -.exhausting work. The idea of attempting to teach a foreign language to children who can barely master their Mother Tongue can seem daunting. Yet young learners are among the quickest to pick up a new language and the most willing to please a teacher.

Up to the age of about six, experts reckon that children are the most receptive to new languages. On the plus side, young children will want to get acceptance and approval from their teacher. They will also respond enthusiastically to what you want to do, and will be happy to try new things. On the down side, their attention span is short, so you'll need to be using several short activities rather than one long one for a lesson.

Teenagers

Anyone who has seen 'The Breakfast Club' knows just how terrible teens can be.

Lethargy, disinterest and apparent amnesia when it comes to bringing books to class are just some of the complaints teachers often make. The one difference between teenagers and young learners is that the former prefer to please their friends, whereas the latter looks for approval from their teacher. Despite this, teenagers can be the most rewarding group to teach. Once you establish some ground rules and they know who the boss is, teens tend to be inquisitive, open to challenges and happy to take on new concepts. When planning lessons, you'll need to find subject matter that isn't too baby-like but that also aren't too adult-orientated. A good way to do this is to start a course by simply finding out what students like, and then designing material around it. Teens rarely get tired of talking about sport, music, the internet and mobile phones.

Adults

As an English teacher, at some point you'll be teaching adults. Your school may decide it wants all staff to learn some English (yes, even the PE guys too), or you may pick up evening work teaching company workers.

Adults tend to be motivated (as they're often the ones paying to learn) and can call on a whole lot more experience than your typical 12 year old. If things go well, classes can be rewarding. Some students are highly dedicated and keen to learn. They come to class armed with questions and won't leave until you've answered them, drinking up knowledge as though it were water in a desert.

That said, if things go badly then adults are far more likely to complain. Adults who are there because their boss put them there are likely to be less motivated than those who are paying for the course. Those who do wish to learn are likely to be far more vocal than younger students if they dislike your approach – you're rarely going to find a Year 6 student going off to complain about your chosen teaching methodology. Teaching adults can certainly help you understand more about your culture, you're going to have more in common with them for a start, but you'll need to be on the ball.

CHAPTER 5: TEACHING THEORY

How do students learn?

OK, so you know who you'll be teaching and who you'll be working with. Now it's time to find out exactly how to teach.

Visit your local library and you'll discover at least one healthily-stacked shelf dedicated to books on teaching theory. If you run your finger along that shelf, a thick line of dust will apply itself to your digit. These books don't get taken out much.

Theory often comes near the bottom of the pile when it comes to teaching, but there are several things worth knowing about how people learn and how best you can teach them. Students who disrupt classes may do so for a number of reasons and knowing some theory helps teachers understand why there is an issue – as well as what to do about it. So don't flick forward to the next chapter just yet.

Many psychologists have tried to understand how the human mind ticks. One of the most memorable was John Watson. Watson carried out an experiment so troubling that today it's remembered more for being so unethical than for the result.

In 1920 Watson, along with his partner Rosie Rayner, began a series of experiments on Albert, a nine-month-old baby. Albert's first task was innocuous enough; he got to play with a white lab rat. He seemed happy to go along with this, until a rather sneaky Watson began smashing a steel bar with a hammer any time Albert touched the animal.

Before long, and hardly surprisingly, Albert wasn't keen on playing with vermin. For Watson, that meant he'd been able to condition Albert to associate the rat with the clanging, and as a result he would become upset any time he saw the rat - noise or no noise. The fact that Albert became terrified of rats, something he had earlier shown no fear of, proved that he had 'learned'.

Watson's experiment worked so well that Albert became terrified of not just white rats but almost anything with hair or fur. Watson paraded rabbits, dogs and even an animal-lined coat in front of the child, each time carefully noting how much Albert freaked out. Perhaps most terrifying of all, one day Watson dressed up as Father Christmas, complete with long white beard, at which point Albert completely lost it.

Watson had assumed that Albert would become conditioned in this way, but was hoping to reverse this process by coaxing Albert into accepting rats again by associating them with sweets and more pleasant sensations.

Unfortunately for Watson, and even more so for Albert, the baby's mother learned of the experiments and promptly put a stop to them. Albert was taken away and Watson never got a chance to complete his tests. We can assume that Albert grew up with a healthy fear of fur, but we will never know for sure as that's the last anybody heard of Albert and his life after those first few months is a mystery.

You may well ask what rats and teaching English have in common. The answer is that Watson's experiment led to the theory of behaviourism. This states that if X occurs because of Y, and you start doing Y to get hold of X, then you've learned something new. Put another way, if a baby gets fed each time it cries, it associates crying with getting food, and so will learn to cry when hungry. On a broader scale, some thought that was how we acquired language, through association and conditioning.

That theory gained some credibility, until Noam Chomsky

turned up. Chomsky argued that if we simply learned language through behaviourism, how could we come up with phrases we'd not heard before? How could Shakespeare have created such moving sonnets if he could only use phrases he'd heard somewhere before? Chomsky had an alternative idea - that we have some innate language sensor inside us and are naturally tuned in to picking up words and structures.

Either way, and the latter way has more followers these days, the best way to learn English is to be immersed in it. Those who are motivated and are surrounded by English tend to quickly pick it up. And if you like the sound of behaviourism, giving students a bar of chocolate for the right answers never seems to produce too many complaints.

Different ways of thinking

Students differ widely in terms of attitude, responses and motivation. One possible reason for this is that we're all wired differently. What sparks fascination in one learner may prompt utter boredom in another.

There are a couple of popular theories about why some people learn best by using different methods. Some students can hold a detailed conversation and use a sprinkling of idioms and phrasal verbs, but give them an exam and they struggle. Others can explain the formula for the Present Perfect Continuous Tense but flounder when you ask them how to order a cup of coffee.

This could be down to one of two theories, the first of which is neuro-linguistic programming (NLP). This says we have one main system and we use this to look at the world. The system is called VAKOG, one of the least memorable acronyms in EFL land, but nevertheless this is what it represents:

Visual

Auditory

Kinaesthetic (movement)

Olfactory (smell)

Gustatory (taste)

When learning, some students will respond to visual aids (flashcards, pictures) while some learn faster through kinaesthetic means (puzzle-solving, activities where students need to move around). While the first three are of interest and should be considered when creating lessons, you'll struggle to find many lessons based around smell or taste.

The other main idea is called Multiple Intelligences (MI). This says we have several intelligences, namely musical, verbal, visual, kinaesthetic, logical, intrapersonal, interpersonal (social) and naturalistic (those that can recognise features of nature).

Creating lessons that tick all of these boxes is tricky, but you should bear in mind that lessons that only focus on one or two of these are likely to be less effective. You can't please all the students all the time, but you can offer a variety of learning activities. Equally, we're not robots and can't be neatly pigeonholed into one of the MIs, so students may well respond well to more varied lessons as they will use more of their intelligences. We aren't suggesting you run through a list of MIs every time you think of a lesson, but we do recommend thinking about how to include a few of these to help give some variety.

Ways of teaching

By now you won't be surprised to learn that for every teaching method there's a corresponding acronym.

Whenever you learn to teach, you'll doubtless be presented with some of these. Great debates rage as to whether PPP is outdated, if TPR works for everyone and if ESA is really PPP in disguise. The good news is that the basics remain simple – keep students entertained and give them a chance to use what they are learning. Here are the main teaching methods:

PPP - Presentation, Practise, Production. PPP is the grand-daddy of ESL methodology. For years it was seen as the definitive way for students to study as well as the ideal way to teach. These days it's often maligned and dismissed by modern teachers as old-hat (they're often the same Philistines who dismiss Pink Floyd as dated).

Briefly, PPP splits a lesson into three parts. The first, Presentation, looks to engage students in the task and offer a model of what is going to be learned, for example a telephone conversation. The Practise part gives students a chance to use that conversation themselves. In the phone conversation example, pairwork would be an obvious choice. Lastly, Production asks the students to come up with their own version of the model. So rather than a phone conversation about booking movie tickets, they could create one based on making a restaurant reservation.

PPP still has its place but it's important to realize that it is *a* way of teaching – it's not the only way. It has many good points but it tends to work best with lower-level groups, not advanced ones. If you think about the phone conversation example, it's a tightly-controlled model that doesn't offer much for advanced students unless we give them a looser reign to create any phone conversation. Another criticism, and it's a justifiable one, is that it can be extremely teacher-centred. The teacher models, the students repeat and then come up with something vaguely similar. Whether learning truly occurs if students only recreate controlled models is a debatable point.

ESA – Engage, Study, Activate. You may well claim that Engage, Study and Activate sound eerily similar to Present, Practice and Produce, and we wouldn't argue with you.

However, the point here is that you can mix things up and have SEA, AES or ESE or ESESA. The limits of lexicography make it tricky to do that with PPP. All ESA means is that you don't have to be rigid with your lessons; if you want to start with a Study activity and follow it with an Activate one, then go right ahead. Taking our phone conversation as the model, you could ask students to begin with a gap-fill of the conversation (a Study phase) then act it out (an Engage phase). After this you could get students to describe pictures of different people (Engage) and then ask them to imagine writing a phone conversation that two of these people may have (Activate).

It can take a little thought to come up with a series of activities that works, but such lessons are usually successful and far more student-centred.

TBL – Task-Based Learning. An increasingly popular method that motivates students by giving them a problem or scenario that they have to deal with. By working through this problem they have to use English and therefore learn without overtly realising it.

An example of TBL would be to get students to imagine they are marooned on a desert island. Present them with ten items (for example: a compass, rope, a lighter, book, shirt, football, knife, spoon, tin of tuna and a mobile phone) and explain that they have to choose only five items for their island. The students work in groups (only speaking English) and then explain their choices to the class. Students then vote based on what they've heard for which items they would take. Students should be encouraged to think practically about how they could use the items; the pages in the book could be burned to make fire, for example.

Students tend to enjoy TBL as they have more freedom. Teachers do need to ensure there is a goal that goes beyond students speaking English. With the desert island example they could be made to use modal verbs when presenting their ideas (have to, must, need, ought to, etc).

TPR – Total Physical Response. Lessons using TPR force students to move around, maybe finding answers in different corners of the room or asking them to piece together information that has been cut up. Obviously a winner with younger students, it also helps students who learn best through kinaesthetic means. If students are learning prepositions of place, you could set up a mini treasure trail in school. Students would have to read the clues (in the corner, under the green box, etc) to complete the route.

CLT – Communicative Language Teaching. This looks for a more authentic style of lessons and uses less grammar than many systems. CLT will often employ role-plays and function phrases (would you like to/in my opinion, etc) to get students using realistic language. When using CLT it's important not to ignore grammar altogether; the point is that with this method you don't get bogged down by it.

Clearly, this is a smorgasbord of styles and a good ESL teacher will nibble on each occasionally rather than devour the same method all the time.

CHAPTER 6: ENTER THE CLASSROOM

So, it's your first day at school. You probably feel the same way you did when you were a student. Lots of new faces, lots of things to remember and an overwhelming urge to hot-foot it back home.

The best way to be confident is to be prepared. Have a broad idea of how your first few lessons are going to go. If you can get hold of a lesson plan or course book beforehand, then wonderful. If not, at least have a 'getting to know you' type of lesson up your sleeve.

My first lesson wasn't one to remember for several reasons. I hadn't been told what year group I'd be teaching, I hadn't been given a course book and I only had a vague idea of how my first lesson would proceed. Within 20 minutes of arriving, the head of department greeted me, said 'Good luck, I hope you enjoy' and vanished.

With that, my first lesson as an English teacher began. I was left alone outside a classroom packed with 55 teenage boys. A lady named Tai from classroom 2/9 emerged and invited me to step inside. The 55 faces had already turned to scrutinise the latest recruit.

So there I stood before a den of baying students. No course book, no direction, absolutely no bloody idea. There can be few things as terrifying as a virgin teacher entering a classroom for the first time. Let alone one entering without a plan.

I walked in and smiled faintly. The head boy sprang up, barked an order, and the rest rose as one and chorused 'Gooood morning tea-cher'. I stood there for a few seconds smiling at their friendly nature when it dawned on me I was supposed to respond.

'Erm, hi, good morning, how are you?' I managed.

'I'm-fine-thank-you. And you?'

'Very well thanks,' I replied, and with that they all sat down again.

What followed will be forever etched upon the memory of each child present, as I stumbled, crawled and tripped my way through my first lesson.

I knew that the ability to relate to things is helpful, so I started by asking if anyone had seen the previous night's football match, which had seen France beat England 2-1 in the European Championships. Given that it hadn't kicked off until 1.45am, it was unlikely many were going to admit to viewing the game, but a few knew the score, so we had an impromptu question and answer session about the match. This seemed to go down reasonably well, so I followed it up with a football quiz. The dozens of faces looking back at me seemed a little dazed by these spontaneous questions.

If teaching were actually a game of football then at this point I would have been the defender hauling down the striker for a last-minute penalty while simultaneously steering the ball into my own net.

They probably felt insulted that I was asking them who Wayne Rooney played for, or that all they had to do was name a Chelsea player, but they sportingly went along with it. The biggest problem was that I couldn't understand half of what they were telling me. It soon became apparent that teaching off the cuff is not a wise move. Preparation is everything.

Following the quiz I muttered a bit, shuffled around a little, and then decided they would be fascinated with details about their new teacher.

'OK, I'm Mark Beales, I'm 32, I am from England. I like reading, writing and movies. What's my name?'

This was a short game.

Once it was over, I tried eliciting the same information from some students, but nothing came back. Foolishly, I then opened the entire floor up so they could ask me anything, absolutely anything at all, about me, my homeland or my interests. The response: complete silence.

At this point it was apparent the students were becoming as confused as their teacher. Games were the last resort, and that particular juncture had been reached several stops back. Taboo, I announced to more silence. After briefly explaining the rules, one boy tried hard to persuade his classmates to say 'grass' by pointing out the window at some trees, while another had the task of describing a 'dog', which he achieved by barking rapidly.

With five minutes of the class remaining, the cavalry arrived in the form of Miss Tai, who it seemed was my teaching assistant. She had been standing at the back the whole time and, in presumably an act of belated mercy, produced the Holy Grail – a course book.

The class opened their books, whipped through some adjectives, and the first lesson was over. It wasn't the smooth and seamless introduction to teaching I had been hoping for, but then the world of ESL is rarely either of those two qualities.

During those first 50 minutes I learned far more than any of those 55 students. In my defence you could argue that I hadn't been told who I was going to teach, or that someone should have shoved a course book into my hands beforehand, but ultimately it came down to being ill prepared.

For the rookie teacher, there are a few golden rules that you simply have to spend time getting right. And here they are.

1) Planning

Planning is the number one key to successful teaching. Get a notebook and jot down how you see your lesson going in your head, from the warmer to the presentation to the summary. This doesn't mean you're teaching by numbers; it just gives you a basic framework and fixes in your head the things that you want students to learn from this lesson.

Once you're in the classroom, lessons rarely follow the notes exactly, but that's fine. If you don't have a plan and simply follow the exercises laid out in the book before you, you won't know where you're going and, more importantly, the students won't know what they're meant to be learning. Simple things like giving each lesson a basic goal (such as 'name the days of the week') and writing this on the board helps the students know what is expected and helps you keep on track.

So, take an hour each week to think about your lessons, go through them in your head and see how they could be improved, and you'll have a far greater chance of making those students listen to what you are saying.

Seating Plans

Planning does not only involve what you are going to teach. Also think about where your students are going to sit. There are two things to consider: how are you going to arrange the tables and chairs and who is going to sit where.

Classroom layout is clearly influenced by the size of your classroom. If you have 40 students in a small room, then your options are limited, but even here you can decide if you want students in rows, pairs or with an aisle down the middle so you can walk around.

With smaller classes and larger rooms, the options are more varied. Traditionally, students face the teacher, but if you're doing a group activity, why does everyone need to be facing the front? If you have students who try and hide away at the back, why not create a horseshoe formation so there is no back?

When it comes to where students sit, teachers often take a back seat. When students are allowed to sit where they please, there is one simple rule – take the ones at the back and place them at the front, and vice versa. More able learners will be good wherever they sit, while those that seek a seat as far from the teacher as possible probably need to be much closer.

A Teacher's Voice

Something as simple as the teacher's voice can be an important factor but it's often overlooked. If you speak at your normal pace and use your normal vocabulary, your students will not have a clue what you are going on about. If you speak at 10 words a minute and only use nouns and verbs, your students will think you a simpleton.

You need to speak in a manner that is as natural as possible, while stressing the key words that will allow students to understand your central message. How you speak can help too: if you're disciplining a student, just the tone of your voice can be enough to illustrate your displeasure. Plenty of teachers have strong accents, and that's no impediment to teaching, but they often try to mellow their sounds so students have a better chance of understanding.

With low-level students, it's wise to write instructions on the board as well, along with several examples of what is required. Sometimes you really cannot go too slowly. Students will generally go along with what you're asking as long as they understand what's expected. If your class doesn't begin working after you finish explaining what's required, there's a good chance they simply haven't understand what you want them to do.

Non-verbal communication can also speed things along. If you want them to listen, cup your hand to your ear, if you want them to write, wave an imaginary pen through the air, if you want them to work in pairs, hold your forefingers out in front of you and bring them together. You get the picture.

2) Writing a Lesson Plan

That piece of paper with lots of boxes to be filled looks daunting. What's a learning objective, what's the learning outcome, what the heck does plenary mean? It's really not that bad, it's just that schools love to have forms. They can wave them under the inspectors' noses when they come to visit.

Some teachers believe lesson plans are primarily for inspectors rather than teachers, and simply go through the motions when writing them. Lesson plans really are valuable though, and the longer you spend on one, the better your lesson will be. That isn't to say that once completed these plans are firmly set out; this isn't teaching-by-numbers. One of the real skills of teaching is being able to adapt; if a class gets it, move on; if it doesn't, how can you explain it differently? If students seem restless, what activity will get them focused? The best lesson plan is an invaluable tool, but it also needs a good teacher to deliver it.

Most lesson plans will have some or all of the following:

Learning objective: This states at the start exactly what the point of your lesson is. This could be 'learning to say the time'. It's a good idea to write this in a box on your whiteboard too, so students have a clear idea of what they're learning. If you want to be fancy you could write WALT (we are learning to…) and WILF (what I'm looking for) before your objective.

Have a look at this learning objective and see if you can spot what's wrong:

'Explain to students how to tell the time'.

The problem here is that this only says what the teacher aims to do. If the teacher explains how to tell the time but the students haven't a clue what he or she is talking about, we can't judge that to be a great lesson. Better to have an objective that states 'students will be able to say the time using 'quarter part/to' and 'half past'. This is good as it's easy to see if learning has occurred. Keep objectives simple, focused on what students will learn, and make them specific.

Warmer: Schools like to put this kind of thing in lesson plans. It doesn't mean you have to play a game every time, indeed you probably shouldn't. A warmer simply means that students are settled, ready to learn and are prepared for what's to come. You could start off by reviewing the last lesson, you could look to engage students with a simple, fun activity, or you could just state the learning objective for the day. Anything that gets students focused and ready will do. In Chapter 8 there are dozens of ideas about warmers and other activities.

Learning Stages: Your school may well call this something different, but essentially this is the body of the lesson. This part should involve students doing as much as possible, as opposed to teachers talking.

Plenary: A funny word that simply means a short activity at the end of the lesson to ensure students have actually got it.

3) Make it real, make it relevant

OK, so in practice how does all that combine to make a lesson? Chances are you'll be presented with a course book that the students are expected to work through. There are many great course books available that make life an awful lot easier. They tend to be grammar-based and fairly formulaic, often starting with a theme, hanging some grammar around it and then developing this with listening and speaking exercises. Nothing wrong with that.

The real trick to good teaching is lifting those ideas from the pages and making them something a student can relate to.

Imagine you have a lesson on Christmas. Your students are Buddhist and don't have a clue who Mary was. It doesn't matter. Begin with talking about festivals in their own country, list them, briefly discuss them, ask questions about them. One of the simplest ways to get students' attention is to slip in the name of their homeland. Just say: 'Now, in China...' and you're guaranteed to have their ears.

As the lesson progresses, be sure of what you need to teach and don't get bogged down by superfluous material. So talk about festivities in China as a warmer, but don't still be there 20 minutes later.

Keep an eye on the lesson plan, even if it's only in your head, and keep things moving along. Once teaching, it's easy to over-explain or hog the limelight, so build elements into your lesson plan that will allow students to participate. Quick, easy comprehension questions ensure students are engaged and also feel they can contribute. Keeping students on-task is a major ESL issue, and you should include students whenever possible. For example, many course books offer basic gap-fill or information-matching activities that can seem monotonous. When you want to go through the answers, put the class in groups and award points for correct answers, give individuals marks for answering, randomly ask students – just make sure everyone is on their toes and has a reason to answer.

When asking questions to a class, don't begin by saying who the question is for. As soon as you mention a student's name, the rest of the class will breathe a collective sigh of relief as they know it's not their turn. Also, they won't listen as carefully to the question as they know they won't be answering it. So ask the question, and then nominate someone to provide an answer.

With a little bit of practice, planning will become second-nature and, once you have everything in place, the actual teaching side of things will also become a whole lot easier - and more rewarding.

Activity: Think of how you could start a lesson on the following topics:

1) Birthdays (learning objective: writing an invitation)

2) Valentine's Day (learning objective: understanding a love song)

3) Hobbies (learning objective: speaking for a minute about free time activities)

4) Animals (learning objective: answering comprehension questions based on a text)

CHAPTER 7: DISCIPLINE

What can go wrong

You are in your classroom, the students are listening, and once you finish talking they quietly complete the task you've given them. Occasionally students may raise their hand and ask a question before continuing with their work.

You stroll around, proud that your students love learning so much. Yeah, ok, now wake up and meet reality.

Sooner or later you will come up against students who would prefer to play up than knuckle down. Even in the best of classes, discipline is always something a teacher needs to be aware of. You may well have just crafted the finest set of instructions since Moses turned up with a few lines scrawled in stone, but if your students don't care you have a problem.

A colleague once pointed out that many Thai schools consist of 'lazy boys and lady boys'. It's a harsh, but often accurate, summary. The lazy boys may outnumber the other variety, but it's the others who are often among the best at English, while also being confident and funny. Their projects drip with glitter and are written in fancy fonts, their pink pencil cases have fur-lining and, come sports day, they're first in line to be cheerleaders, shaking silver pom-poms. You can't help admire students who have so much confidence and who aren't afraid to stand out, especially in a system where standing out and individualism is often frowned upon.

Cultural differences can sometimes make things awkward and good teachers will be aware of the potential pit-falls. In some Asian cultures, smiling is a mechanism that allows everybody to get out of tricky situations with their reputations intact. So if you're disciplining and a student and he/she is smiling, it could be their way of coping (alternatively, they could just be smirking at you). Many students will not be used to doing group work and so may be reticent to join in at first: many Asian schools prefer the chalk-and-talk method where students take a far more passive role. Students will often say they understand when they haven't a clue, as this is the answer they think the teacher wants to hear and they don't want to be the source of any conflict. For this reason, specific comprehension questions work far better than asking 'do you understand?'

Other students often lack motivation. In a school system where legally everybody has to pass, you can understand why. Work your socks off, study hard and do your best, and you'll get about the same score as the kid snoozing next to you. In many countries, English is rarely spoken at home, and so students may see little point in learning. Motivation is therefore the key to successful teaching. Getting your students to see the importance of learning for learning's sake, and not simply to pass tests, is the trick.

Corporal punishment

Some countries still permit corporal punishment – most do not. When you join a school you'll be given a discipline code, and you can be pretty sure that beating a student with a wooden stick won't be one of the recommended strategies.

Local teachers, on the other hand, sometimes bring out the stick with very little prompting. New teachers sometimes find it hard to come to terms with seeing their students whacked, but in many Asian cultures it's something that has gone on for decades and no amount of cotton-wool legislation is going to stop that. Some schools have their very own head of discipline. He (it's going to be a man) will have his own office, his own set of rules and probably his own stick, possibly laced with barbed wire. Mr Surit was one such man. He rode around my former school on his yellow scooter with the kind of expression exclusively made by those who ride Harleys and have tattoos of Satan on their forehead. Even the other teachers steered clear of him.

I once saw Mr Surit with a line of boys. He paced up and down for a few moments yelling in their faces. When he grew tired of yelling, he produced the dreaded stick. Each boy assumed the position and down came the stick with a crack onto the student's behind. With his friends nearby, each child would try and stifle a yelp but few managed to take their punishment in complete silence. Mr Surin drew back his stick, released, and then waited for another student to face him. And their crime? They'd been found wearing the wrong colour socks.

Such attacks don't happen every day, but taps on the wrist or clips round the ear still go on, so get used to them. That said, as a foreign teacher you don't enjoy the same ability to bend/disregard the rules. Students also know you can't touch them, and so you need to take discipline seriously.

Start strong

You are the teacher. You are not their new best buddy.

That's a good start to controlling your classes. Many teachers begin by wanting to win over students with games, rewards and laissez-faire lessons. Students enjoy this, realise you're 'cool' and not like those fussy local teachers. At some point you need to actually teach, but the students are still in the game zone and don't fancy it. And no amount of cajoling and 'come on guys, let's work now' is going to do it. To them, you are the teacher who plays games, not the teacher who teaches.

Starting off strongly is crucial. During those first few days you don't just get to size up the students; they get to size up you. Begin with a set of clear rules that everyone understands. Then introduce a set of clear consequences if anybody breaks the rules.

Display the rules somewhere prominently and refer to the poster every time one is broken. Many students actually prefer to have consistent and understandable rules to follow.

If students do step out of line, it's not enough to merely threaten them with punishment. If the punishment doesn't materialize, students quickly realise you're bluffing.

Punishments can take many forms, and they tend to be graded. Here are some ideas (going from minor to serious).

1 Write the student's name on the board.

2 Tell the student he or she is to miss break-time and will have to work.

3 If the student does not attend their detention, call the parents.

4 If the student continues to be disruptive, arrange a meeting between the Head of Department, the parents and yourself (and be sure to get your Head of Department on your side ahead of time).

Top Tip: Always be aware if you have a lesson right before a break. Often the threat of missing break time is sufficient for good behavior to return. Suggest that the whole class may miss their break because of one student's actions and you're virtually guaranteed success.

Dealing with problems

Sooner or later one of those rules is going to be broken. Whatever the issue, it's important that you are consistent when meting out punishments. If your best student has just trampled on

Rule 3, then he is in as much trouble as anyone else. Students have a heightened sense of fairness, and if you're not seen as consistent then you'll soon lose their respect.

So given these scenarios, what would be your response?

1) Nut is hard at work – surreptitiously reading his comic under his desk. Do you:

a) Stop the class and announce to everybody that Nut has something he'd like to share with everyone.

b) Stare at Nut, eyes popping out like those in a Tom and Jerry cartoon, and yell 'Nut, Noooo!'

c) Walk over to Nut, take the comic away and tell him firmly to get on with his work.

Answer: c) Humiliating your students or losing your temper rarely wins the day. You should also talk to Nut in private after the class.

2) Juan is talking quietly to his friend while you're trying to explain something. Initially, do you:

a) Walk towards his desk and make eye contact with Juan.

b) Stop what you were saying and glare at Juan from the corner of your eye.

c) Get Juan to repeat what you just said.

Answer: a) In the first instance, sometimes just a teacher's physical presence is enough to make a student realise he or she's erred. Walking towards his desk forces Juan to pay attention, and also means you don't have to actually interrupt the lesson. For all you know, Juan may have been discussing his work with a friend.

3 Yuto just won't pipe down. This is the lesson you spent a whole afternoon preparing, and does he appreciate it? No. So, do you:

a) Berate Yuto for his lack of human decency and declare that you would rather poke burning rods into your eyes than teach him for another moment.

b) Stop the class and take 5 minutes to explain to everyone the meaning of the word 'respect'.

c) Quieten Yuto down and then talk to him after class on his own.

Answer: c) While a) may often be the most tempting solution, diatribes don't work, and probably won't be understood. Importantly, in many cultures it's the person who loses their temper who loses the argument, so count to ten and think of another option.

Answer c) is also good as it doesn't interrupt the lesson, doesn't humiliate Yuto in front of his friends and gives you the chance to clearly explain to Yuto what the problem is. While it's important to maintain discipline, it's important to do it quickly and effectively, so you don't waste valuable teaching time.

Learning Difficulties

Many schools have problems dealing with students who have behavioural problems. In some countries, these students tend to be left to cope in mainstream classes, largely because there is no alternative.

In developing countries, there are few options if your child is autistic or has a behavioural disorder. Parents often don't like to admit their child has any issues and insist on keeping him or her in mainstream education.

If you get the chance to talk to the teacher you're replacing, ask them if there is anyone to look out for with Special Educational Needs (SEN) in the class. Otherwise, you could be in for a shock, as I was during my first few days with a new class. We were playing a quick vocabulary game to review some new words, and all seemed to be going well.

Part of the game was a hangman-like quiz where students could choose a letter and try and guess the word. After a few turns, one of the quieter students, who tended to spend his time drawing musical staves, took an interest. His hand shot up and it waved furiously around in the air.

'Hmm, yes, OK Gun, do you want to have a guess?' I asked.

Gun nodded fervently and replied 'Five'.

'OK Gun, this is like hangman, so we're really after a letter,' I explained.

A little crest-fallen, he went back to scribbling crotchets. A minute later we were onto a new word, and again Gun's hand was up.

'Yes, Gun, do you know the word?'

'15', came the reply.

Gun could actually do most of the work, the challenge was persuading him that it was worth his while. Gun really wanted to just write music. His love of writing crotchets and quavers extended to actual songs, so any time I used a song he would be up dancing around the room, and no manner of persuasion was going to get him to remove his disco shoes.

Gun was harmless, but other students can be far more troublesome. Big, a 12-year-old boy, was one such student. His teacher was an English woman in her mid-20s who had never taught before. Big's English was good, but each lesson he would test his teacher to see how much he could get away with. The teacher handled things pretty well, until during one afternoon class, she'd had enough.

After telling him repeatedly to take his book from his bag and at least open it, she raised her voice and told him, in so many words, to pull his finger out. Now nobody in the school spoke to Big like this, not even the Thai teachers, but nobody had passed this information on to his English teacher.

Big stood up, screamed at the teacher in Thai, tried his best to rant a little in English, then finally threw into the air the few papers he had bothered to take out of his bag. He ran out of the classroom and downstairs, where I was walking past.

Big stood alone, oblivious to anything, literally shaking with rage. I approached and asked what was wrong. Big scowled at me before launching a salvo of expletives towards me in his native tongue. Unfortunately for Big I knew what he was saying and so put on my best authoritative tone and got him to calm down. Big did seem genuinely sorry about the insults he'd sent my way, or possibly sorry that I'd understood him. We sat on the stairs and chatted for a while about his problem, and after 10 minutes, all was well with the world. Big wasn't a bad student, he just had certain needs that weren't going to be addressed well by this particular school. Thai teachers shrugged and labeled him 'autistic', but that tends to be a term that's banded around for any problem child.

If you do have students such as this, then do your best to find out the full picture. Teaching those with SEN is a completely different job from teaching ESL, and so you'll have to find ways that work for you and your student, and don't impact on the amount of time you have left to teach the rest of your class. International schools may have specialist teachers for this type of situation, but that's the exception rather than the norm. A good option is to get the student professionally tested to see if there are any underlying problems, but tread carefully; not all parents want to admit there is a problem.

So, having gone through what to do when things go pear-shaped, here's a list of what you can do to regain control.

Top Ten Discipline Tips

1. Write five lines up on the board. Each line represents a minute of game time at the end of the lesson. Every time a student is naughty or noisy, simply rub out a line. This works well with primary and some secondary classes. They soon get the message. Alternatively, draw a line that represents a fuse. Erase a little of the line each time there is a problem. If there is no more fuse left, there are no games at the end.

2. Get the following translated into the student's mother tongue (L1 is the technical term). Give an English and L1 version to any troublesome students. Tell them to take it home, get their mother and father to sign it, then return it to you.

Dear Mother and Father,
I was very naughty in class today. I was rude and disobedient. I was loud and disrespectful. I wasted my teacher's time and your money. I am very sorry.
Signed:_____
PS: Please sign below so I can return this letter to my teacher.
Father:_____
Mother:_____

Obviously, this can be adapted to suit the circumstance. This shouldn't be done for minor problems, and shouldn't be done too often. Students, especially troublesome ones, tend to be adapt at avoiding punishments, so if you do use this be sure that someone calls the parents to confirm they actually received this letter (and to check the student hasn't just faked those signatures).

3. Get a list of the students' names. When they do something well, award a merit point. When they do something bad, deduct a point. At the end of each month print off a 'certificate' for the student with the most points in that month. At the end of the year you could offer a prize for the student with the most marks overall. Only ask students for answers if they are sitting quietly and not yelling out. Competition works well in most countries, and this method ensures that less-able students can also take part. I used this idea regularly, making sure that a variety of students won the prized certificate. One of the main features of discipline is that it should be reward good behavior and focus on the positives.

4. Rather than berate a student who is talking too much, ask him/her a question relating to the lesson. This quickly focuses his attention on the task at hand and ensures you don't waste time admonishing the student.

5. The famous yellow and red card system. Get some coloured cards and every time a student is bad, present them with a yellow card, football-style. Two yellows equal a red and a punishment. Works especially well in all-boy schools.

6. Encourage students to speak English only in the classroom. Keep a list of who speaks the most English and who speaks L1. At the end of each week give a small reward (sweets, etc) to the one who has spoken the most English. A variation of this is to hand out prize tokens to students who you hear using English outside of the classroom. Every month, you can then have a prize draw and offer a small reward to the winner.

7. This is ideal if you have a lesson just before a break. For any troublesome students, write their name on the board. If they continue to act up, put a cross next to their name. If they get three crosses they have to give up their break time. Take them to the staff room and give them extra work. A simple break-time task that takes no time to prepare is to give the student a picture or topic and ask them to speak about it for a minute.

8. If a class is finding it hard to get settled, get them to do a writing exercise, such as a journal. Give them a topic, such as 'what I did last night' or 'five things I have learned this week'. Bear in mind that noisy games at the start of the class tends to make students hyper, whereas a writing or reading game tends to focus the mind more. Leave the noisy games until the end. Then it's the next teacher's problem, not yours.

9. Whatever you do, do not embarrass or ridicule a student.

10. Don't compete with noise. Sometimes talking quietly about something of interest will ensure students listen.

CHAPTER 8: HOW TO MAKE IT INTERESTING

Knowing what you need to teach is one thing; knowing how to teach it is something else. A good teacher is like a magician, capable of randomly producing things from up their sleeve to keep their audience attentive. Always be conscious of how you could lift a lesson with one of these games or tasks. Sometimes students need to get away from their books and just use English for a specific purpose, and games such as some of these below add a competitive edge that gives students all the motivation they need.

This chapter explains the various activities that can be used to engage with students. Think of these as some of the tools you need as a teacher, and be ready to adapt them as necessary for your classes. Some of these ideas may seem as though they are just designed as warmers at the start of the class, but they can easily be used in the main body of a lesson to check students are on-task, and to ensure they remain interested.

Warmers

Warmers are an important part of a lesson. They aren't just there to fill time while you figure out what page they're on today. A simple warmer should be either used to review the previous lesson or set the scene for the day's class. If done well, students become interested and are then easily led into the main task.

Here are some ideas for warmers, but if you find yourself with ten minutes of spare time at the end of a class, they're just as good as time-fillers. There are hundreds of games and variations of games for teaching English, so try and find ways to adapt these ideas – or ignore them altogether and come up with your own.

Memory game – The teacher says: 'I went to the market and bought a pig.' The first student repeats and adds another object, and so on until someone forgets the order. Choose students at random to ensure they all have to memorise the list, and make sure they don't write anything down. It's impressive how far the list can go before someone trips up. A good way to remember is to link the different items through visual images, so if an elephant, car and apple are mentioned you think of an elephant squeezed into a car munching on an apple. As the teacher, it's wise to write down the list so you don't forget!

Verbs and adverb - Give students coloured paper strips. On one colour they write a verb and on the other an adverb. Put students in pairs or teams. Student A picks a verb and an adverb and acts it out. Student B guesses which of the words the student has chosen and is awarded a point for each correct one. Examples could include 'walks nervously', 'swims crazily', 'talks quietly', brushes his teeth carefully'. The teacher should model this first so students are clear what is required.

Initial letters – Give students a letter and tell them to write as many words starting with that letter. For higher level groups, make it verbs/adjectives/food/animals etc starting with that letter.

Colours – Give students a colour and tell them to write down as many objects that are this colour (blue hat, blue table, blue book don't count).

Quick on the draw – Two teams. Show one student a word and tell him/her to draw it on the board. First team to guess the word gets a point. Examples: food, household objects, office objects, animals, verbs.

Snake game – give students a word and tell them to make a new word that starts with the last letter of the first word. Students continue to write as many as they can within a time limit. Example: e*gg*, *g*oose, *e*lephant, *t*eapot. For more action, use a small ball to throw between students and make this a speaking game. This ensures everyone is awake or they run the risk of a ball landing on their head. For advanced students limit the words to certain groups, such as sport or food.

Hangman - An old favourite and much-maligned by many, but it can still be a useful way to review vocabulary.

In the Mix – Write a long word on the board. Students then have to make as many words from it as possible. Example: spaghetti – it, past, get, hit.

Noughts and Crosses – (or tic tac toe) A great game that is hugely adaptable. Fill each square with a letter, which is the answer to a question. Two teams take turns to pick squares. It can also be used for grammar-based activities. For example, the teacher writes infinitive verbs in the squares and students must change them to the Present Continuous and put them in a sentence. To make it harder write '+', '-' and '?' next to each verb, to indicate you need a positive, negative or question form. Similar games work well for past and perfect tenses, as students often have trouble remembering irregular verbs.

Easy as ABC - Write the alphabet on the board. Pick a letter and a category and ask students to name something starting with that letter. Example, A and fruit – apple. B and verb – bring. With wide, open themes you can ask groups of students to find something to fit each letter, eg, food, countries or animals.

For more advanced student give a question for each letter, such as 'three animals starting with A', or five verbs starting with S'. Once students get the hang of it, they can ask each other (but they must be able to answer the question themselves or you'll get lots of '20 adverbs starting with X').

Truth or Lies? - Give five statements, and say two of them are true. For an introductory lesson, it's good to write about yourself; for other classes you could pose general statements. Students can ask questions to discover which they think are correct. Once completed, students can then write their own five sentences and quiz each other.

Spelling tennis – Two teams. The teacher shouts out a word and points at one student, who must say the first letter of the word. Point at a student from the other team, who must say the second letter, and so on. Model this first with an easy word such as 'dog' and they'll understand far quicker than if you explain it. This can be a fun game and get rowdy, but there's limited educational value so don't play it for too long. As an alternative, bring a small ball in. Throw the ball to one student, who has to spell a word (1 point), translate it (1 point) and use it in a sentence (1 point). Note that pointing may be culturally insensitive in some countries, so you may want to say the students' names.

Touch game – Two teams. Pick two students from each team to stand up. Give them an order, such as 'touch your nose', 'hold up three pens' and award a point to the fastest. To make things interesting, try 'give me 10 dollars' or 'touch that tree outside'. This can get pretty noisy, so it's a good one to play at the end of a lesson.

Taboo – Give one student a word which he/she has to explain to the class. Give them two other associated words which they are not allowed to use. Obviously, you can make this as simple or as complex as you wish. It's an ideal way to force students to use improvisational techniques to achieve their goal. For instance, the word could be 'beach' and the taboo words may be 'sea' and 'sand'. The student could say something along the lines of 'this is a place we go to at the weekend to relax. It's hot and you can lie on the warm, golden floor'.

Mimes – write a word on a slip of paper and show it to one student, who must then act it out. First team to guess wins a point (examples: sad, happy, wet, angry, laugh).

Spelling race – Two teams. Select a student from each team, who are then handed a marker pen and stand near the board. Say a word and the first student to correctly write the word on the board wins a point. For advanced students, make them write it in a sentence. Try to keep this for small classes, as with bigger numbers too many students are left with nothing to do.

Categories – Write a category on the board, such as music genres, footballers, England, Things in the Sea. Then write associated words, with spaces for each letter. Students guess the answers and can ask questions if they are stuck. Here's an example: England 1) _ _ _ _ _ (queen), 2) _ _ _ _ _ _ _ _ (football), 3 _ _ _ _ / _ _ _ / _ _ _ _ _ (fish and chips). The teacher will need to give clues throughout, so there's a strong listening element to this game.

Scategories - Write several subjects on the board, going across horizontally: animal, film, food, drink, boys' name, and then have a student pick a letter. Write the letter to the left of the first subject. Students then work on their own to find words for each category that start with the given letter. For example: B – animal (bat), food, (banana) colour, (brown) city (Boston). Some teachers call this game 'stop the bus!' as this is what students have to call out when they've finished. We've no idea why.

Mobile phone - Two phones – fastest student to text a given word gets a point. Schools often ban phones so this may be better for adult classes (be sure they turn them to silent once finished!)

20 questions – The teacher thinks of an object/person/place and students have 20 questions to figure out what it is. It may be an old parlour game, but it forces students to ask yes/no questions, and you'd be amazed at how they're able to guess the most obscure things.

Countdown – Choose four random numbers 1-10 and then four numbers from 10, 25, 50 and 100. Pick a three digit number then ask students to get the number. Make sure they explain in English. Review 'add, multiply, divide, subtract' before you start! You can also do this with letters if you divide up vowels and consonants, then ask students to make words from them.

Sentence change - Say a sentence then change one part of it. Students have to say the new sentence. For example: 'He works in Madrid twice a week.' Teacher: 'you – Student: 'You work in Madrid twice a week.' This is a substitution game that can be used to test all kinds of tenses. Write down the words you want to focus on beforehand, as it can be tricky to think of new ones off the cuff.

Apples and Bananas – good with smaller classes. Students stand in a circle and have to count in sequence. However, if the number is a multiple of 7 they must say 'banana'. If the number is a multiple of 5 they must say 'apple'. For example: '1, 2, 3, 4, apple, 6, banana…8, 9, apple, 11, 12, 13, banana, apple, 16…'. Those who get it wrong are out and have to sit down. Continue playing until you get a winner.

Bingo – This is a good listening game. Tell students to each write a 4x4 grid in their books. Then show a selection of vocabulary on the board. Students chose 16 of these words to write in their grid. The teacher then randomly calls out the words and the first student to get a line of four wins. Or you could just do it the traditional way and use numbers.

Adverbs/adjectives - Two teams write lists of five adjectives and five adverbs. They then swap lists. One team has to act out the other words using one adjective and one adverb, while the other team has to try and say which of their words they are miming. For example: 'he is running quickly', 'he is laughing crazily'.

Where is it? - Send one student outside then hide an object in the classroom. The student returns and one other student from his team has to give directions to find it. This works well if you're teaching prepositions of place.

Word Association: Say a word and the next student has to say any word linked to it - football - Arsenal - London - Big Ben - clock. See how long they can continue without hesitating or repeating a word.

Blockbuster – Draw a grid of letters on the board. Each letter represents the first part of an answer. Each team takes turns to pick a letter and the teacher asks the corresponding question. The aim is to create a link from one side to the other. Try and come up with questions based on a topic your class has been studying or on a general theme.

Longer activities

Story telling – divide the board into nouns and verbs. Ask students for five nouns and five verbs. Then get them to write a short story using all ten words. Point out the stories must make sense, otherwise students will create any old mess just to include the target words. Be sure to use words students have recently learned.

Running dictation – Write ten numbered sentences on a piece of paper and stick it somewhere outside the classroom. Students work in teams. One student from each team runs outside without pen or paper and memorises the first sentence. He/she comes back and tells his friends. They all write the sentence down. The next student shows the teacher the first correct sentence and can then run outside to read the second sentence. The first team to correctly write down all the sentences wins. If learning a grammar point, leave some target words out and make the team complete them. This is an energetic game that tests all kinds of skills (memory, spelling, teamwork). It also brings out the devious side in every student so watch out for those looking to smuggle pens outside or those who want to nip out without showing you the last correctly-written sentence.

Drawing – Tell a story to students using plenty of adjectives and nouns. Students make notes in small groups. Students then draw the story on large coloured paper. This is a good game for younger learners.

Describing – Pairs: Students draw a bizarre-looking monster but don't show it to anyone. Students then use 'have got' to tell their friend what it looks like, and their friend draws what they are told. For example, 'it has got three heads'. At the end they check to see if the pictures look alike. Use this when you're teaching 'have got/haven't got' or the third person singular equivalent.

A Day in the Life of…- a good way to get students using their imagination. Base this on a character they've been studying, or use interesting examples such as an astronaut, Mr Bean, a policeman. Set a word and time limit. With advanced group, ask students to imagine they are the character and get them to write in that person's tone. This is called an empathic response.

Journals – It's useful if students have time to write down their own thoughts at least once a week. Set aside 10 minutes for your class to jot down what they have done this week or what they have learned. Encourage them to express their feelings too, rather than simply create a diary-type list.

Picture this - Show different groups pictures of a situation and ask them to write a story based on the picture. At the end get each group presents its results. Another way to use pictures is to show an image or a still from a movie (Mr Bean is perfect) and ask students to say what is happening.

Grammar Gun: Write a text with several mistakes in (with the errors preferably focused on a point they're learning). Students work together to circle all the errors. Once finished, a student reads out one paragraph at the front. If he/she misses the mistakes they are 'shot' by another student with a toy gun. Naturally, if you're teaching English in a war-torn country, you may want to skip the gun element and get students to fervently shout out 'no!' each time a mistake is made.

Cartoons – white-out the text from a popular cartoon strip and make some copies. Then ask students to come up with new dialogue and a storyline. They can then act this out in groups at the end.

Debates – propose an idea to the class, say 'school uniform is pointless'. Split the class in two; one half agrees and one half disagrees. Working in groups, students formulate opinions and then present their arguments. The class ends with a vote. Check out www.idebate.org for some thought-provoking topics.

Spelling it out – Give a mock spelling test with ten words. Go through the words to check spelling and comprehension. Next, ask students to make up a story using these words, in any order. Make sure you use words that you have covered already, and preferably include some that students have difficulties with.

Role-play - Hand out cards to pairs of students explaining various situations. For example, students have to make a complaint in a shop, apologise for stepping on someone's toes or ask permission to go home early. This is a great way to practise function phrases, which are a crucial part of spoken English. Give students time to prepare (unless they're elementary, don't let them write anything), then act out each scenario in front of the class.

CHAPTER 9: GRAMMAR – THE BASICS

The verb 'it' and other disasters

Ask any ESL student what they want to learn about English, and most will say 'I want to improve my grammar'.

There is a fixation with many students, and some teachers, that perfect grammar is essential in order to communicate in English. And it so isn't.

If you ask me 'the bank where?' I'll have a good idea of what you mean. The grammar may be horrible but you have communicated something to me. And communication is the name of the game.

Grammar is the cement that holds language together. Without it you can still build a brick wall that will generally do its job; it just won't be a very strong one.

Before my first Business English courses began, we had to interview the students to assess their levels. One woman with short, swept-back hair and glasses was going to be taking my course seriously.

'So what would you like to learn during the course?' I asked.

'I want to learn about the 12 tenses.'

'Wow' I thought, 'there are 12?'

There are indeed a dozen, although when teaching you'll do well to touch on more than half of them.

If you're a native speaker of English, the chances are you've never had to think about what the Present Perfect Continuous Tense looks like. Trust me though, you do know it and you have been using it (and reading it). If you're not a native speaker, then congratulations, you've probably had to learn it all before so this will be child's play.

When teaching it is imperative that you know what you are talking about back to front, right to left, bottom to top. If you aren't completely sure of something, you will have a hard time explaining it clearly to someone. So take time to fully understand what may seem obvious until it truly becomes obvious.

You'd be amazed how some teachers bluff their way through the day with zero understanding of what they're talking about. During an observation class, I once saw a teacher demonstrate how his understanding of grammar was about as effective as an elephant with chopsticks.

'OK class, settle down' he began "today we are going to study the verb 'it'."

I looked up from my notebook and assumed I had misheard.

But he continued: 'The verb "it" can be used in many ways. "It is hot, it is dangerous, it is 8 o'clock". Now, copy these.'

Most of the class was unaware of the grammatical homicide being committed before their eyes, but a few smart students were soon displaying furrowed brows as they tried to understand.

Just to clarify, 'it' is a pronoun. It always has been and always will be. The moral here is clear: know your grammar and your terms.

Another teacher, who lasted barely more than a month, knew what a certain verb was; he just didn't have a clue what to do with it. He approached me one day and, with complete honesty, confessed: 'so what's the verb "be" all about then?'

'Well, it's an auxiliary verb, you know, the "is/am/are" stuff.'

'Mmm, yeah I see. So why do they call it "be" if it's "is/am/are"?'

'That's the base form.'

'Ahh', it seemed as though the penny had dropped. But it hadn't dropped entirely; it was hovering on a precipice.

'So why do they say "to" be, what's wrong with the "verb be"?' he continued. The penny never quite made it over the edge, and the teacher was on his way before long.

Accordingly, being a native speaker doesn't mean you know how English works, it means you know what sounds right and what sounds wrong. Being able to explain why something is right or wrong is the trick.

All English words are broken up into different groups, according to the jobs they do. Here are the basic terms, which are called Parts of Speech:

Nouns: These are objects, people, places, or abstract notions. If you can put 'the' in front of the word, you're probably looking at a noun. Examples: horse, pen, house, Mexico, idea, information.

They come in a few shapes and sizes. Common nouns are things like 'pen', 'hand' and 'phone'. Proper nouns are the ones that have capital letters (England, John), abstract nouns are things you can't put your finger on (intelligence, enjoyment, pleasure, idea), collective nouns treat a group as if it were one (herd, council, flock) and compound nouns (where two nouns come together to form a new one (classroom, train station).

To make nouns plural, we normally put an 's' on the end (so it's one horse but two horses). However, there are exceptions. Words that end 'ch', 'sh', 'x' or 's' tend to have 'es' added to the plural form (boxes, watches, matches). Being English, there are of course even more exceptions, in the form or irregular nouns (woman/women, sheep/sheep, tooth/teeth).

Teaching nouns is pretty straightforward work as visual aids can often be used. It can get tricky when students want to use 'much' or 'many'. To do this, students need to understand that all nouns are broken into two categories: countable and uncountable. Countable are, unsurprisingly, ones that you can count (burgers, boys, schools) and others are not (ice, money, hope). An easy way to teach this is that **u**ncountable nouns use m**u**ch, which both happen to have the letter 'u', while countable nouns go with 'many'.

Verbs: These are action or doing words. Examples: run, think, kick, understand. Verbs change according to when the action occurred.

English has three varieties of verb tenses: Infinitive (go), Past Tense (went) and Past Participles (gone/been). To make things simpler, teachers often refer to these as Verb 1 (infinitive), Verb 2 (Past Tense) and Verb 3 (Past Participle), and we'll do that here too.

The exception to all this is the Modal Verb. These are used to give advice, suggestions or orders (should, ought to, must). They never change their spelling (apart from the past of 'have to', which is 'had to') and they also don't care if the subject is 'he/she/it.

Students often have a hard time remembering that while 'have to' and 'must' broadly mean the same thing, their opposites 'don't have to' and 'must not' are very different. Oh, and you can't use 'must' in the past tense.

Auxiliary verbs, sometimes called 'helping verbs' are tiny little things (do, is, have) but are crucial as it helps us make all kinds of sentences.

One more thing that's important: verbs are either transitive or intransitive. Transitive (trans meaning 'cross') verbs are followed by an object; the other ones aren't. This is why 'Liverpool won' is a sentence but 'Liverpool beat' is not.

Adjectives: These are words that describe a noun. They usually come before the noun (the *red* car). The exception is if you use the verb 'be' (the car is *red*). Examples: thick, fast, thin, handsome, clever, long.

When teaching adjectives, you'll need to be aware that if there is more than one in a sentence, they come in a particular order, which is why we say the 'big, new, Brazilian yacht'. In case you're ever asked, this is the order they should come in:

1: opinion: ugly, fast fascinating
2. size: small, tiny, big
3. age: old, young, ancient, new
4. shape: square, rectangular, circular
5. colour: blue, white, red
6. nationality: English, Mexican, Australian, Vietnamese
7. material: silver, wooden, plastic
8. purpose: drive-through restaurant, fishing boat

You may also be asked to deal with comparatives and superlatives. A good way to do this is to ask two students to stand up and write the word 'tall' on the board. Elicit that students need to say 'Student A **is taller than** Student B'. This little formula goes 'Subject + 'be' + adjective-er + than + object'. This works perfectly with monosyllabic adjectives. With polysyllabic ones, we need to add 'more'. Keep those two students standing and now write the word 'handsome' or 'beautiful' on the board. Now students will need to say 'Student A **is more handsome than** Student B'. The formula for this is 'subject + be + more + adjective + than + object.

Comparatives work when there are only two items. To make superlatives, we need three or more subjects, so this is where you ask a third student to stand up. Repeat the same activity as before, but now we're clearly trying to reach 'Student A is the tallest' and 'Student B is the most beautiful'. Similar rules apply: adjectives with a single syllable get 'est' tagged on the end while longer words require 'the most' to be added.

Pronouns: These take the place of nouns to stop sentences sound terminally dull.

These are broken down into various sections:

Subject pronouns: (I, you, we, they, he, she, it)

Object pronouns (me, you, us, them, him, her, it)

Possessive pronouns (mine, yours, ours, theirs, his, hers its)

Reflexive pronouns (myself, yourself, themselves, himself)

Adverbs: A little more tricky. Adverbs usually describe verbs and typically end in –ly. Examples: quickly, gingerly, well. They tell you where, when or how something was done.

Just to confuse things a little, not every word ending in –ly is an adverb (lovely is an adjective) and there are plenty of adverbs that don't have –ly (often, seldom, tomorrow).

Adverbs also break down into various groups. And here are the main ones. You could give this to students and ask them to add some more examples.

Manner	well, quietly, excellently
Degree	very, quite, really
Time	soon, in a minute, recently
Place	there, under, here
Frequency	sometimes, never, always

Teaching adverbs can be fun. A classic game is to write a series of activities on one set of cards and then adverbs on another. Students then have to pick one activity and one adverb, then mime it. So this could involve 'brushing your teeth crazily', walking down the road slowly' or 'picking your nose intensely'. Remember that adverbs have peculiar habits and can appear at various stages of a sentence, so be aware that students may have difficulty with this.

Prepositions: A word, or group of words, which shows how other words are connected. Examples: 'Send me two boxes *of* paper', 'We will meet you *in* reception *at* 2pm.' English has prepositions of time (*at* 2pm), prepositions of movement (go *over* the bridge) and prepositions of place (it's *in* the corner).

With prepositions of place, use spot the difference games and get pairs of students to work out differences using adverbs. For example, 'in my picture the boots are under the table, but in your picture they are under the chair'.

Conjunctions: These are words that link other words together and also explain actions. Examples: so, and, because, until, but. Make a poster and stick it up in your classroom, as these words are crucial to sentence building and it is useful for students to have a visual reminder nearby.

Activity: Try this out. Read the following sentence and identify a noun, a verb, an adjective, an adverb and a preposition.

The clever student quickly understood the concept of grammar.

Answer

Nouns: student, concept, grammar

Verb: understood

Adjective: clever

Adverb: quickly

Preposition: of

With elementary classes, it's worth taking your time to ensure students understand and can identify these terms. Sometimes they won't know what they are in their own language, so offer lots of examples until it sinks in.

Once they are comfortable with the terms you can introduce some of those 12 dreaded tenses. Most languages have the

Present Simple, Present Continuous and Future Simple, and so these are relatively simple to explain. Others, such as the Present Perfect Tense are absent in some languages and so are generally harder for students to comprehend. Whatever you do, do not simply teach these as formula to be remembered; think of ways students can use these tenses in meaningful ways. Rote learning is not the same as understanding.

Tenses

Present Simple

This tense is used to talk about something that is true now, something that is always true or something that happens regularly.

Examples

Peter is in Sydney (true now).

Sarah studies Chinese at the weekend (happens regularly).

Phuket is the largest island in Thailand (always true).

How to make

Positive: They   like   Liverpool

       Subject + Verb 1 + Object

Negative: They   don't   like   Liverpool.

       Subject + don't/doesn't + Verb 1 + Object

Question: Do   they   like   Liverpool?

       Do/Does + Subject + Verb 1 + Object?

With the Third Person Singular (he, she, it) we add an 's' if the sentence is positive. If it's negative or a question, we use 'does'. So that's why we say 'she like**s** Liverpool' and '**does** she like Liverpool?'

Get students familiar with the idea of adding an 's' when they see he/she/it sentences. Not only do Thais not pronounce 's' at the end of their words, but Thai verbs know their place and never change, regardless of what tense is used.

How to teach

Ask students to write sentences about their family, their house, or what they do every morning. Make sure the focus is on writing the correct verbs. This usually works well as students are asked to talk about a variety of people, so the 'he/she/it' structure often appears. Once finished, students could swap their books and mark each other's work.

Activity:

Tick the sentences which use the Present Simple Tense.

1. I use the internet three hours each day.

2. He has worked here for three years and has been deputy chairman for one year.

3. The company has written to the supplier asking for more information.

4. We hope to arrange a meeting for next week to discuss the proposal.

5. The rain has stopped.

6. My manager has gone to Europe for a business meeting.

7. Here comes the new engineer.

8. I hope to be there tomorrow to discuss the problem of component over-heating.

9. My computer isn't working again.

10. Have you been to the new office?

Present Continuous/Progressive

A quirk of English (as if there weren't enough) is that experts can't even agree what to call some tenses. Thus some books will say Present Continuous while others insist on Present Progressive. It's the same thing.

This tense describes actions that are happening now or about now. In some cases it can also refer to future events.

Example: We are eating fried grasshoppers. (at the moment)

        I'm seeing my friends this weekend (future event)

How to make

Positive: He   is   listening to his iPhone.

      Subject + be + verb-ing + Object

Negative: He is not (isn't) listening to his iPhone.

      Subject + be + not + Verb-ing + Object

Question: Is   he   listening to his iPhone?

      be + subject + Verb-ing + Object

The idiosyncrasies of English spelling have been known to trip some students up here. There are two things to be aware of with –ing verbs. If a verb ends in 'e' then we usually cut the 'e' and add 'ing', as in 'they are *making* pizza'.

If the verb has a vowel and a consonant together, we usually spell the verb with a double consonant (swimming, running, stopping). If there is a double vowel or double consonant cluster, then we just add –ing (looking, drawing, punching). As with many things in English, there are exceptions to the rule.

  Students have a tough time remembering the word 'consonant' so often I just use 'vowel' and 'not a vowel'.

How to Teach

This is one of the most interesting tenses to teach, and also one of the easiest. Here are some ideas:

- Play a short video clip, then stop and ask students 'what is he doing/wearing/thinking/looking at/eating?'
- Bring in a variety of pictures from magazines or websites. Put students into small groups and ask them to write as many sentences as they can using the Present Continuous Tense.
- Split the class in two. Ask one student to come forward. Write down a verb or action that only the solitary student can read, such as 'ride a buffalo'. The student then has to act out the verb until someone makes the sentence 'he is riding a buffalo'.

Activity

1) Make Present Continuous sentences from these examples.

1. John / read / report   Answer: John is reading the report.
2. David / wait / for a phone call.
_____
3. I / make / a proposal.
_____
4. The manager / stop / overtime.
_____

5. The engineer / help / the IT department.
_____
6. The bus / run / late
_____

Past Simple

As you might expect, this deals with things in the past. More specifically it deals with things in the past that are now finished. We indicate something is in past by changing the verb.

Example: I *bought* four goldfish yesterday.

How to make

Positive: Richard liked   Sarah.

      subject + Verb 2 + object

Negative: Sarah didn't   like   Richard.

      subject + didn't + Verb 1 + object

Question: Did Sarah   like   Richard?

      Did + subject + Verb 1 + object?

The good news for students is that for about 80 per cent of verbs you simply add –ed to create the past form. The bad news is that the most commonly-used verbs happen to be in the other 20 per cent.

How to teach

A simple warmer is to draw a noughts and crosses, or tic tac toe, board and write nine infinitive verbs in the boxes. Divide the class into two groups. A student from each group must then pick a verb and make a Past Simple sentence using the verb.

For less able groups, just make them say and spell Verb 2 correctly. For more able groups, add positive, negative or question mark signs next to the verb, to show what kind of sentence you are looking for. Use irregular verbs (ones that aren't spelled with –ed) with higher level groups.

Keeping a journal is an excellent way for students to write on their own and to develop their own thoughts and opinions, and for the most part they'll be using the Past Simple Tense. Obviously, any worksheets on historical events work well here and news reports often use this tense. Blank out the verbs or ask students to write a follow-up report, still using the Past Simple Tense.

Future Simple Tense

In English there are two main ways to talk about the future, using 'will' or 'be going to'. Thankfully, there is very little for students to get wrong here, although some insist on leaving out the verb 'be' and only use 'going to'.

Use 'going to' when there is more certainty about the outcome or when a decision has been made some time before.

Use 'will' when you are expressing an opinion or when the idea is made at the moment of speaking. Sometimes you can use either form.

Example

I *will* have the soup please (decision made at the moment of speaking.)

When I get a pay rise, I'm *going to* buy a new house (talking about future plans.)

How to make: (with be going to)

Positive: We are going to see a movie this evening.
      Subject + be + going to + Verb 1 + object

Negative: We aren't going to see a movie this evening.
      Subject + be + not + going to + Verb 1 + object

Question: Are we going to see a movie this evening?
      Be + subject + going to + Verb 1 + object?

(with will)

Positive: He will go and play video games later.
      Subject + will + Verb 1 + object

Negative: He won't go and play video games later.
      Subject + will not (won't) + Verb 1 + object

Question: Will he go and play video games later?
>   Will + subject + Verb 1 + object

How to teach:

An obvious way to get students speaking is to talk about their plans for the weekend, or what they will do after school. For written work, students could talk about they want to do when they leave school, or with higher level groups, they could talk about their ambitions and hopes for the future. Remember that younger students find it much easier to talk about themselves than abstract ides such as 'my hopes for world peace'.

Don't spend too much time forcing students to differentiate between 'going to' and 'will'. As long as they know there's a difference and when to use which form, that should be sufficient.

Present Perfect Tense

And so we come to the one tense strikes fear into the mind of every English student. The tense that some think is about as simple as doing a Rubik's Cube blindfolded. Yet it really isn't that bad. The Present Perfect Tense can be used to describe several situations, which is why some find it tricky. In a nutshell, it's used to talk about things that started in the past and continue now, or for things that are important now.

Example: She *has been* to Africa ten times.

How to make

Positive: The tigers   have   escaped from the circus.
>   Subject + has/have + Verb 3 + object

Negative: The tigers   haven't   escaped from the circus.

Subject + hasn't/haven't + Verb 3 + object

Question: Have the tigers escaped from the circus?

Has/have + subject + Verb 3 + object?

How to Teach

A good first lesson is to talk about a student's favourite subject – themselves. Get a list of activities or experiences they may have done and go through them. Make some feasible, others bizarre, for example: 'Have you ever eaten pizza?', 'Have you ever seen a ghost?' If you're feeling creative, cut the questions up and get students to pick one out of a hat.

You can develop this so students then go on to create their own questions. At an early stage, a simple 'yes, I have' or 'no, I haven't' is an acceptable answer. Don't ask them to expand on their answer or they may have to switch tenses and then it gets messy.

We use the Present Perfect Tense here as it is talking about a past event that has importance now, because we are talking about. Importantly, when it happened is not mentioned. You can't say 'have you ever seen a ghost last week?'

The Present Perfect Tense tends to be among the more difficult of tenses for students to learn, often as there is no equivalent in their native language, and also because it involves having to think about the past and present together. However, there are many good activities that can help students overcome any trepidation.

Students can read news reports, which often use the Present Perfect Tense to give a sense of immediacy ('a train has crashed'). This helps to show how an event in the past (the train crashing) is linked to the present (I'm telling you about the crash now).

There are several songs that use this tense, notably U2's 'I Still Haven't Found What I'm Looking For'. Blank out the Past Participle (Verb 3) and see if students can fill them in as they listen.

They could then discuss things that they also have not done yet, and which are likely to come true.

The words 'yet', 'just' and 'soon' are often linked to this tense. 'Yet' is used with negatives and questions (I haven't written the letter yet / Have you finished yet?) while 'just' goes with positives (I have just finished). Again, simple gap-fill exercises are a good way to check understanding here.

Passive

Using the passive voice is frowned upon in most writing circles, but students of Business English can't get enough of it. The passive voice is usually taught at pre-intermediate level and above and so you will come across it at some point. Put simply, the active voice is where the subject is doing something. The passive voice is used where the subject has something done to it.

Example

Active: Lions *eat* rabbits (the lions are doing something, eating).

Passive: Rabbits *are eaten* by lions (the rabbits don't do the eating)

How to make

Positive: Cars   are   made by machines.

  Subject + be + Verb 3 + object

The cars aren't doing anything, they're passive. It's the machines that are doing the work, but here we want them to be the object of the sentence.

Negative: Cars aren't   made   by machines.

  Subject + be + not + Verb 3 + object

Questions: Are cars   made by machines?

  Be + subject + Verb 3 + object

How to teach

The above example (lions eat rabbits) is a good way to explain the passive voice.

Write it on the board and ensure everyone agrees with the sentence. Then write 'rabbits eat lions' and ask if that is also ok. Once students understand it's definitely not ok, ask them to try and explain why.

Worksheets on inanimate objects work well (i.e. the history of jeans, a story about the Titanic) as they tend to be written using the Passive form.

OK, so that's a rundown of the most important elements of English grammar. There are a few more tenses but they are all just combinations of the above, so get these mastered and you'll be fine.

The bad news is that English is an incredibly mixed language; a hotch-potch of rules and structures borrowed from all corners of the globe. For every rule there seems to be an exception. For every definition there's a 'but…'. The good news is that most ESL students will only need to worry about the above. Non-defining clauses and the like come much later.

CHAPTER 10: THE FOUR SKILLS

Being able to use English well means four things need to be mastered – reading, writing, listening and speaking.

Try and get a mix of these in all your lessons. Usually listening is taken care of indirectly as you'll be talking for some of the time, and if you have a course book there's going to be reading involved. That's two out of four taken care of. Think of ways you can introduce the other elements – even if the lesson is based on a reading text there are many ways you can ensure all four elements are used. The temptation in many classes to merely focus on the reading and writing, after all that's what will be in their exam. However, your job is to get students to communicate, not merely understand formulaic grammatical patterns.

This chapter runs through each of the four communication skills and offers a few ideas about ways of teaching each one.

Reading

You should always give your students a reason to read. The mere joy of picking up a book and being able to enjoy a range of literature isn't going to cut it with a generation who'd rather be on Facebook or playing online games.

It's fine to have a reading class, but make sure students produce something at the end of it, whether it's a book report or an empathic response (remember that one, we did it earlier?) With higher level groups, you may find students are happy to grab a book and dive in, but with lower levels they usually need some persuading.

Reading, like any activity, needs to be introduced properly. Begin a class by presenting your students with a chapter from Harry Potter and telling them 'read this' will result in blank stares. Ask your students to tell you five words associated with Harry Potter and you've got the start of a lesson.

Once you have your five words, you can show students a picture (on paper or computer monitor) of a scene from one of the movies. Get them to tell you about it and predict what is happening (they can do this even if they don't know one wizard from another). After this, ask them to read a short extract from the book that relates to the following scene and see if their predictions were correct. Once that's done you can get them to pretend they are a character and ask them to write a journal about what happened to them and read it to their friends.

And there you have it, one ready-made, boil-in-a-bag, lesson.

As with all classes, begin by engaging students, then introduce the topic and give them a task. Once the task is completed you can expand things a little and get them to produce their own work. If you've been paying attention, you will also have noticed that we use all four communication skills here: the students listen to the movie extract, tell you their predictions, write down their character's journal and read the chapter.

There are a few other things you should bear in mind:
- Firstly, think about the level of your students and the text you want them to read. If possible, use authentic texts but don't worry about slightly simplified stories, as long as it sounds natural, it'll do. In general you want to aim for a level that is very slightly above where your students currently are. They should be able to read at least 80 per cent without diving for a dictionary every

other line. This will breed confidence and provide some opportunities to learn new words.

- Make sure it's something you can get them interested in. A school once decided to introduce a new reading programme for all students following an inspector's negative remarks. They parachuted in a programme straight from the USA and handed it to their EFL students. Suddenly 12-year-old EFL students in Southeast Asia were being asked to study material designed American primary students. The topics were far too childish and the texts far too simple, so by the time one teacher had finished handing out the books to the class the first student had finished his. The level was wrong and so was the subject matter – a student in Southeast Asia just can't get that excited about the origins of the Stars and Stripes.

Even here, there is a way to salvage the mess. The student may show complete apathy for the Stars and Stripes book, but may well be interested in his own nation's flag, so get them to research it and present their findings to the class. Once they finish the set book, you could also ask the students to design a new national flag and write down why they had chosen particular colours or symbols.

- Get them interested. Show pictures, give clues, read the book aloud with some actions – do anything that will persuade students reading can be fun.
- Give them a task. Teaching experts with lots of letters after their name talk about intensive and extensive reading. Intensive means reading for a purpose; extensive is more about reading widely and for pleasure. Either method is ok, but higher level students tend to prefer extensive reading as it's more focused around their level and offers more opportunities for expansion.
- Set a time limit. Given the choice, students would happily sit with a dictionary and pen by their side, searching

for every word they have doubts over. After 20 minutes there will be a page of translated words scribbled across the text, but ask them what the story is about, and they won't know. You don't want a text where every other word is unknown to your class, but equally you want a text where some words are new. Encourage students to work out meaning from context, not from dictionaries.
- Be creative. With a little preparation, you can use almost any reading material with any class. Presenting your class of elementary students with a Shakespearian sonnet may seem like madness, but ask them to pick out the continuous verb forms or negative structures and suddenly they're presented with something achievable.

Here is the skeleton of a reading class that you could easily adapt for your students.

1. Begin with a game that introduces new vocabulary (stick words up around the room, ask them to try and build a story with those words, or predict how they may be used).
2. Once students have read the text, get feedback. How many people were there, who is the narrator, did they like it, who is it written for?
3. Follow-up activities are where the fun really begins. Tell students to create a role-play based around the characters, get them to predict what will happen next, ask them to discuss a central theme or give them a scenario based around the text that they can work on in groups.

The beauty of reading is that you can find material from anywhere. Grab some take-away menus when you're passing by your local Indian, take a handful of train timetables from the station, snatch some tourism leaflets from the town hall. You can ask simple comprehension questions or get students to ask a classmate for specific information that is on the leaflet or menu.

You may feel newspapers are too difficult, and some certainly are. Regional papers and tabloids (in the UK at least) offer simpler language than broadsheets and may be appropriate. If nothing else, you can explain the style of a page, asking what job the headline does and how the page is laid out.

Here is a basic reading comprehension passage. You could find similar texts almost anywhere, and then base questions around them. Be aware that you may need to simplify language for lower-level students, but be sure to retain the overall meaning of a text.

Michael Jackson

1 Michael Jackson was born in America on August 29, 1958 in America. He started singing with his brothers when he was 11 years old. He was the youngest singer in this group, The Jackson 5. They sold millions of records and made Michael Jackson a star. After he began to sing solo in 1971 he became even more famous.

2 His 1982 album 'Thriller' is the best-selling album of all time and has sold about 110 million copies. His other albums include 'Off the Wall', 'Bad', 'Dangerous' and 'HIStory'. Some of his most famous songs include 'Billie Jean', 'Beat It' and 'I Just Can't Stop Loving You'.

3 Michael Jackson was one of the first black singers to 'crossover' to a world-wide audience. His concerts were famous, and many people loved to see him dance. He influenced many of today's stars.

4 Michael Jackson won 13 Grammy awards, had 13 number one singles and sold more than 750 million records. He is the third best-selling singer ever, after The Beatles and Elvis Presley.

5 He wrote the song 'We Are The World' in 1985 with Lionel Richie, which helped poor people in the U.S. and Africa. It sold

nearly 30 million copies sold and raised millions of dollars for famine relief.

6 Michael Jackson was also famous because of his bizarre person life. He had brown skin when he was a boy but when he was older his skin became whiter. He claimed he had a skin problem. He also changed the way his nose, eyes and chin looked. He used to have a chimpanzee as a pet and lived in a huge home called the Neverland Ranch, which had amusement rides, a zoo and a cinema.

7 Michael Jackson died on June 25, 2009. After his death was reported, the internet slowed down. During the week after his death, on the website Ebay 14 of the best 20 selling albums were by Michael Jackson.

8 Jackson died 18 days before he was due to start a series of concerts in London. A movie was made that shows rehearsals for these concerts. The movie is called 'This Is It' and was very popular, making more than $261 million in cinemas around the world.

Questions

1) Michael Jackson began singing in a group

a) before he was a teenager.

b) when he was a teenager.

c) before he was five years old.

2 A 'star' in the first paragraph means

a) something in the sky at night

b) he became a famous person

c) he liked famous people

3 How many 'Thriller' albums have been sold?
a) 110 million
b) 1982 million
c) 750 million

4 What do you think a 'crossover' singer is?
_____

5 Has Michael Jackson sold more records than anybody else?
Yes ____
No ____

6 The song 'We Are the World' helped people who
a) were hungry and had no money
b) had no homes and were hungry
c) had no jobs and no homes

7 In paragraph 6 'bizarre' means
a) unusual
b) interesting
c) change

8 Michael Jackson's skin colour
a) became darker as he grew older.
b) stayed the same .
c) became lighter as he grew older.

9 After Michael Jackson died

a) the internet became faster and people bought his CDs.

b) the internet became slower and people bought his CDs.

c) the internet became faster and people didn't buy his CDs.

10 Michael Jackson died

a) after his London concerts had begun.

b) prior to his London concerts.

c) during one of his London concerts.

Lastly, here are some ideas for materials, and which levels they are best suited to.

Beginner

Reading menus

Identifying labels

Reading road signs

Identifying people from descriptions

Identifying website and email addresses

Telephone directory

Elementary

Reading directions to solve a problem

Following instructions

information-sharing for timetables

Reading email messages

Creating text messages for a phone

Reading directions on a street map

Lower-intermediate

Cut up a story and put in the correct order

Television timetables – matching with people's preferences

Advertisements

Reading simple notices

Reading emails

Intermediate

Newspaper articles (tabloid)

Websites

Holiday brochures

Identifying business-related faxes/messages

Matching newspaper stories and headlines

Identifying parts of a diagram

Post-intermediate

Identifying genres

Non-fiction

Instruction manuals

Movie reviews

Horoscopes

Dating ads – matching people

Proficient

Letters to a magazine

Editorial comments in a newspaper

Fictional novels
Broadsheet newspapers
Book reviews
Biographies

Advanced
Newspaper reports (broadsheets)
Scientific reports
Magazine features
Autobiographies
Novels, various genres

Writing

Let's start with the basics. Writing needs to be legible, otherwise what's the point? We may exist in a world of computers and keyboards, but most students will still be using notebooks and pens, so they need to be able to produce words that are recognisable. While this is an important skill, some schools are more insistent than others on 'good' handwriting. A school I once heard of took this to rather an extreme and decided that all students should be able to write in a joined-up fancy style. When the students were taking an age to finish the first activity of a particular lesson, the teacher went over to check on their progress. They hadn't yet got past writing the date, as they were trying hard to master the 'F' in February and apply the appropriate loop or swirl. Fancy writing is an admirable skill, but worry about the basics first. Students may well write letters in a peculiar, long-winded manner simply because nobody has ever showed them an easier way. If you spot poor writing, watch as the student writes to see if he or she is holding their pen at some bizarre angle.

Of equal concern is spelling. English is maddeningly inconsistent when it comes to spelling and so it's a place where students often come to grief. You can't blame them; who'd imagine that 'through, bough, cough, thorough, thought and tough' would all use 'ough' – and all sound different? Mobile phones can also be blamed for modern spelling atrocities, and it's not uncommon to see 'how r u?' and 'Thx 4 yr help' in notebooks. Extensive reading is the best way to improve spelling and word awareness, rather than endless spelling bee tests that use plenty of words, but rarely put them in any type of context.

Writing can take many forms, and it's good to create lessons that show students the differences. A letter to your bank manager is likely to be pretty different from one to your girl or boyfriend, while an e-mail to a mate is probably not written the same in tone as a job application.

Writing e-mails, letters, resumes or reviews are highly stylized. Each one has things the other does not (Dear Sir/Yours Faithfully, etc). Get students to practise different genres and make sure they are aware of the differences. Writing such as this is handy as it's 'real' – you can use that resume or you can send an e-mail to a friend. Writing for a purpose is therefore important. If students decide they want to write to a famous person, for example, why not send the letter to the subject? My class once wrote a letter to Queen Elizabeth II, introducing themselves and their country. I sent off the best examples to Buckingham Palace, and a month later a note arrived from the Palace thanking the students for their interest and wishing them well. The class could instantly see the effect that their classroom efforts had out in the real world and were delighted (not half as delighted as the Head of Department, though). Along with particular forms of writing, there are also certain phrases, or functions, that we use depending on the message we want to get across. Encourage students to learn phrases, rather than individual words. So, if you students are writing a letter to give advice they would find the phrases 'why don't you + Verb 1', 'how about + Verb-ing' and 'I think you should + Verb 1' rather useful.

As well as somewhat formulaic letter-writing, creative writing can be just as useful, and often more enjoyable. Remember that younger students find it hard to think beyond things they can see, so a topic on 'my hopes and dreams' isn't likely to come to much. You'll need to set the scene for creative writing, offering some ideas to get the ball rolling.

If you're fortunate enough to have access to computers, then contact a foreign school or college and set up a pen-pal exchange (maybe pen-pal's not the right term any longer, maybe 'mouse-mate' sounds better).

Ideas for writing tasks

- Go through a controversial news item on a website or newspaper. Ask students to write to the newspaper with their opinions on the piece. Remember that most news items can be used for most levels; you may just have to adapt them a little.
- Give students a text with many spelling mistakes, or one with no punctuation, and ask them to fix it. Here's an example you can use:

My Journal

Saturday May 28

It is Saturday today. I happy because it is my birthday. Every Saturday I to go and see my friends in Chicago.

Today I excited because I will have a birthday party with my friends. My friends am from England, america and australia. They friendly.

One of friends is Peter. He has got big, blue eyes, and long, curly hair. One of my friends is Janet. She have got a big smile. I sometimes play tennis with her. When we play tennis it is funny.

> Every Saturday we meet and to eat food together.
>
> There are a good restaurant in Chicago called 'Tony's Ribs'. There are many tables in the restaurant and there is many candles on the table.
>
> After we eat we go and watch a movie.

The useful thing about such texts is that you can adapt them. If it's too tricky, keep the mistakes to just the verb 'be', if it's too easy add some extra problems. Tell students how many mistakes there are as this gives them a target (the above has 12 errors)

- Ask a class to write an instruction manual for an everyday machine (writing an e-mail, making a cup of coffee, doing the washing), as this will help with conjunctions and writing about sequences. Ensure students begin each instruction with appropriate conjunctions, such as 'firstly', 'then', 'next' and 'finally'. Get someone to act out the sequence at the end to check each stage is complete.
- Think of some 'day in the life of…' scenarios and get students to write about these.
- Set aside time each week for a Journal. Ensure it's not simply a 'got up, brushed my teeth, went to school' affair. Encourage students to say what they felt about certain activities or events. Younger students don't tend to have scintillating social lives outside of school, so you could limit entries to what they did at the weekend. It's also a good way to practise the use of the past tense.
- There are three basic kinds of writing tasks: controlled, guided and open writing (though you may see them called different things at times). Here are some sample lessons for each.

Controlled Writing

This involves giving students help, direction and model sentences. Often used with lower-level classes, the teacher may simply present one sentence (John is walking to work) and ask students to convert this into a similar form (John and Geoff are walking to work).

Alternatively, you could try this lesson.

Stage 1: Rubric: 'Put these words in the correct group. Group A has capital letters, Group B does not (you could dictate the words first to add a listening element)' The words: *london, spain, train station, library, bill gates, town, city, chelsea, the beatles, pop music.*

Stage 2: Rubric: 'Now add punctuation to these words'.

The words: *Stop, I couldnt hear, she wont like this, are you coming, Liz is older than John*

Stage 3: Rubric: 'Look at the following story. Work in pairs. Student A: draw a circle around every word that needs a capital letter, student B draw a star next to every word that needs punctuation. When you finish, swap papers and write in the correct punctuation and capitization.

'john and liz went to london last week john didn't want to go but liz wanted to go shopping when they arrived john couldn't stay in the shops for a long time because he was bored he thought im going to get a coffee and he left liz in the shops outside he was crossing the road when somebody shouted hey john be careful a cars coming a man pushed him to safety john said thanks very much wait a moment I know you youre david from my old school they went to have a coffee and john enjoyed his day when he saw liz later he asked what did you buy and liz replied I didn't buy anything it was all too expensive I don't like london anymore'

- **Guided Writing**

This offers a little more freedom than controlled writing, but still keeps a pretty tight hold on the work.

Instructions: Place students in groups of three. Each group is given six pictures, which show different sequences in a story. Each picture has been cut up and numbered (but not so 1-6 is the correct order). Ask the students to first arrange the pictures in a logical order. With groups of three, each student could have two pictures.

Next, ask students to use the Present Continuous Tense to write down what is happening in each picture. Not all sentences have to be in the Present Continuous as this would be unrealistic. If necessary, use the first picture as a model: 'The man is walking in the park. There are many leaves on the ground.'

Ask students to write down the remaining sentences.

Collect the best answers and write them on the board, to show one possible answer. Example: The man is walking in the park. There are many leaves on the ground. (2) The man is brushing the leaves into a pile. (3) The man is putting the leaves into a basket. (4) The man is carrying the leaves in the basket. It is very windy. (5) The wind takes the leaves, they are flying in the air. (6) The man is very angry because all the leaves are back on the floor again!

Once complete, put students in different pairs and tell to think of another story with six parts. They have 10 minutes to draw six pictures that depict the story (no writing). They then join with another pair of students and swap pictures. The students have to write sentences describing the other pair's pictures. Stress that the focus is mainly on the Present Continuous Tense to ensure the task remained short, interesting and manageable. Of course, you can use any grammatical structure you like for this.

- Or, you could adapt this:

TEACHING ENGLISH

The text below comes from a tourism website, but some of the language has been simplified and changed in order to test certain features, such as 'there is/there are'. The table below ensures that some choices will have an effect on what comes later, for example 'delicious' can only go with 'dinner cruise', which in turn can only go with 'on the river'. With (7), if students choose 'at times', they would have to then pick 'but it is possible to use' and so on.

Authentic text taken from www.bangkok.com.

Bangkok (1)	is often is often referred to (2)	as called (3)	one of the most exciting (4)	cities countries towns (5)	in the world. (6)
Although At times (7)	Bangkok's traffic vehicles (8)	can be terrible, may move slowly, (9)	there are there is but it is possible to use (10)	motorbike taxis a skytrain taxis (11)	if you want comfort. if you don't mind weaving in and out of traffic! that have meters and can take you anywhere. (12)
There are There is (13)	a range of things to see and do, many attractions, (14)	such as for example, you can try (15)	an exciting a relaxing a delicious (16)	Thai massage ride on a tuk-tuk dinner cruise (17)	on the river. in a spa. on Bangkok's busy streets. (18)

Students have to write accurate sentences, choosing the correct option each time.

- Give students a map of London (or any other major city). Ask students to write brief sentences about where different tourist attractions are in London. Model sentences would include: 'The Houses of Parliament is near the River Thames, and so is Cleopatra's Needle. The Imperial War Museum is on St George's Road. Marble Arch is on the corner of Park Lane and Bayswater Road.'

Students would then be shown how to link these into more complex sentences. A model sentence here could be:

'The Houses of Parliament is near the River Thames while Westminster Abbey is situated between The Houses of Parliament and Westminster Cathedral. Just behind Westminster Cathedral is Buckingham Palace, and behind the palace is Wellington Arch.'

The rubric would then tell students 'using this model as an example, write longer sentences about London's tourist attractions.'

- It is important that students can arrange their sentences into meaningful ideas that connect with each other. Here's a Harry Potter-themed lesson that focuses on conjunctions – words that are essential for linking sentences and thoughts.

Rubric: 'Make the two sentences into one sentence by using a conjunction. Choose a conjunction from the box.'

Example You couldn't see train platform 9 3/4. _____ It was real.

You couldn't see train platform 9 3/4, but it was real.

1) Harry's parents were killed. _____ Albus Dumbledore looked after Harry.

2) Harry was nervous about the first day of school _____ He didn't know anybody.

3) Harry did not like his Potions class ___ The teacher was scary.

4) Harry thought he was in trouble when Professor McGonagall caught him on the broom. _____ The professor liked Harry and said nothing.

5) Normally students were not allowed in the Forbidden Forest, _____ Professor Snape allowed Harry to enter

7) The Quidditch match went on as planned _____ The rain that made everyone wet.

8) Harry went to find the Sorcerer's Stone. ____ Professor McGonagall's assurance that it was well protected.

9) Harry and Hermione fought the giant dragon. ___ They killed the giant dog.

10 They went home for tea. _____ They killed the dragon.

| in addition therefore   because   despite   after   but |

These examples offer some brief ideas, but it's important for teachers to think of what will appeal to their own students and then adapt or come up with fresh ideas.

Open Writing

As the name suggests, this has fewer boundaries than the controlled and guided writing. Here are some examples:

- Find a picture you think is suitable as stimulus for a free writing activity. Provide a list of questions designed to focus and initially direct the writing. Ask students to say what they think has happened or will happen in the picture.
- Get students to read about a survey and then write a paragraph to sum up the information.
- The following lesson is based on a mining accident in Chile, but it can easily be adapted. In this case, 33 miners were trapped 700 metres underground with little food or water.

Show students four pictures that depict the rescue. Go through the pictures in groups. Students write down what has happened in each picture. One student can write down on behalf of the group. The teacher provides a model version featuring the students' work for others to write out.

Follow-up activity 1: You are the manager at the rescue site. You have to write a report about how to rescue your miners.

First, you need to send food and water to keep the miners alive. Next, you need to design a rescue capsule and decide where to dig. If you dig too close to the miners, the rest of the mine may collapse. If you dig too far, you won't be able to see them.

Decide how many holes you want to dig. Too many holes will make the mine unstable, too few means you may not reach the miners. Decide where you will dig and how big the hole will be. How will you bring the miners to the surface safely?

Think about the problems the miners will have; how will you help them?

Follow-up activity 2: Imagine you are the brother or sister of one of the trapped miners. Write to the mining company saying how you feel and asking them to make the mines safer. Think of three questions to ask the company.

Listening

Listening is perhaps the hardest of the four communication skills. It's not like reading or writing, where you can go back and check what is going on. Listening is a one-stop shop: you get to hear something once and then it's gone forever.

Listening is also the one thing students do naturally every time you speak, so there are plenty of opportunities for them to get used to it. The chance to hear a native speaker talk is great; it's even better if you've got something interesting to say. Guest speakers are something of a luxury but there are definitely some folk living near you with a story worth listening to, and who would be happy to tell it.

As well as live speaking, a lot of lessons make use of recorded material on CDs or online.

Typically there are two stages to a listening exercise. The first time students listen to find out what's going on in general and the second time they listen to pick out specific information. It's important to point this out to students as it allows them to focus on particular things each time they listen, rather than worry about having to understand every word. Students often panic when listening and, once they've missed the first answer, then fret and miss every other answer. Point out that students need to continue listening actively, rather than let the noise wash over them.

Here are some ideas for listening lessons:

- Recorded material from course books is fine, but why not make up your own scripts and get them recorded? The advantage here is that you can tailor it to where you live and include student names or other local detail. You can also control precisely what students listen out for. You can use correct English or natural English, which is likely to have more of 'erm', 'ah' and 'yeah'. The tricky part here is to present natural English that students may hear, but you may not necessarily want them to replicate it in their own speech. Enlist a fellow teacher and make up some conversations. Provide students with comprehension questions and other follow-up activities.

- The internet is a blessing for teachers. If you happen to have a computer and wifi in your classroom, there are some superb listening exercises on YouTube and other sites. Be sure students don't only listen but have some follow-up activity to complete.

- Short movie clips or excerpts from television shows offer authentic language and plenty of chances for predictive exercises and feedback. Pause the clip as you go along and ask questions or give students questions in advance that they can answer as they listen. Put the questions in the same order as the extract, unless you want to make it really challenging.
- Course books come with audio CDs or links to online resources which have gap-fill or jigsaw-type activities. These may not be natural but they do allow students to listen for specifics. Students tend to need listen two times to a track.
- When we listen, we are often thinking not only about what is being said but also how we are going to respond. If we didn't do this, there would be long, awkward silences in the middle of our conversations. So anticipation is also an important part of listening. Try reading out the following to a class and have them write in the blanks (they don't need to write down what you say).

Hi Peter, how are you?
_____
I'm ok, but I do have a small problem.
_____?
Well, there is a girl I work with and I really like her, but I am shy.
Ahh, _____ ask her if she wants to go and see a movie?
No, I can't do that. She might say no.
If _____. Understand?
I guess so. Do you think she will want to go out with me?
I'm sure she will. So are you going to ask her or not?

- Set challenges that students need to complete through listening. For example, let's say you have just completed some lessons on prepositions of place. You could then use a spot-the-difference activity, similar to the one below, to test this.

Draw two trees in boxes labeled A and B. Next to the tree in Box A draw a dog and in Box B draw a horse. I would then say: 'in picture A there is a dog next to the tree, but…'. I would then elicit a similar response to describe picture B.

If needed, repeat several times using different images. Once students are comfortable with the idea, put them in pairs, facing opposite each other. Each pair has two different, but similar, pictures.

Provide as much scaffolding as required and model at least one example.

Then say: 'OK, now I want students A to tell students B one thing about their picture. Student B, listen and then say if your picture is the same or different. Try and find 10 differences. Circle any difference.'

Constantly monitor pairs to prevent the use of L1 interference. Telling students how many differences there are helps set a definable target. Of course, the internet can provide you with hundreds of 'spot the difference' pictures of varying levels of difficulty. This is a great exercise as it employs speaking and listening skills, with a defined goal for all students.

- Here's a simple lesson based on weather forecasts, ideal if you want to review numbers or days.

Introduction: Ask students 'what is the weather like today?' Hand out pictures showing different types of windy conditions and elicit or give related vocabulary: windy, breeze, gale and hurricane.

Next, distribute flashcards with the following words: 'light breeze', moderate breeze' 'fresh breeze' 'gale', 'strong breeze', 'violent storm' 'hurricane'. Students arrange these in order, from the weakest to the strongest.

Tell the class they are going to hear people talking about what the weather will be like in the next few days – better known as a weather forecast (see the text below). With elementary classes, it's best to start with a general achievable task and then focus on specific detail. This way students also feel they are able to listen and achieve something.

Firstly, ask 'what will the weather be like on Wednesday?' Once we've established it's going to be windy, say 'OK good, now listen again and note how many 'wind' words you can hear'. Once that's complete, you can start to get more specific, and ask 'Now, listen and tell me what time people have to stay in their homes'.

And now here's the weather forecast: *Here is the forecast for Wednesday. The weather will be very windy all day, starting with 25kph gales in the morning and possibly reaching 80kph gusts in the afternoon. We advice people to stay indoors from 2pm-4pm to be safe .There is a chance we may be hit by a tornado in the early evening.'*

Once that's been completed, students can delve a little deeper. Hand out a grid (see below). Tell students to listen and tick all the boxes that the weather forecast talks about.

TEACHING ENGLISH

Forecast: *Good morning, this is the weather forecast for Monday August 10th. Today we have calm winds of only 5kph, but we are going to issue a special weather warning. Due to a high pressure system, we will be experiencing winds of about 25kph on Tuesday afternoon. This will continue all night until Wednesday morning, when we expect a strong breeze of about 80kph. The winds should then slow down during Wednesday afternoon, when you may only notice smaller trees swaying slightly. We advise people to stay indoors on Friday evening though. A major storm is due to arrive that could damage property, cars and anything else that is outside.*

Wind Speed	Descriptions	When?
_____	Smoke shows the movement of the wind	Today (Monday)
_____	The wind moves paper	Tuesday afternoon
35kph	Small trees start to move	_____
55kph	Difficult to walk	
80kph	Trees fall	_____ _____

100kph	Danger to your house	_____ _____
120kph	Danger to everything	_____ _____

Music – how to strike the right chord

From Peru to Poland, everybody loves music. Songs are just about the finest arsenal you have in your teaching bag, so make good use of them.

Music is not only enjoyable but it uses natural phrases and slang, can inspire discussions and is a great way to get students speaking (or warbling). Collect songs and accompanying worksheets as you go along and you'll soon have a song for every occasion, or at least every tense.

There are a few things to remember when using music. Think about whose music you will play. The Beatles may well have been the biggest group of all time, but your students may not know Lennon from Lenin. They may see it as music their grandparents told them about, so it's important to engage students first and explain just how damn good John and Paul were. It's wise to find out what your students do like listening to, and find songs they may be more receptive to. Whatever their preference, always go through the lyrics of any song first and skip those songs that talk about 'my bitches' and 'blow'.

Think about presenting the lesson, don't just announce 'listen to this song' and hit play. Sometimes even just the intro can be enough as a warmer. Play the first 30 seconds of a song and ask students what genre it is, how it makes them feel, even what colour they associate with it. You'll be surprised how enthusiastic students are to do this. This kind of warmer is also recommended as helps break down the idea that listening is 'hard' as you begin with a small, achievable task and can then build on it.

Here are a few ideas for how to use a song:

1. Play the song without giving students the lyrics. In pairs, ask them to note down four verbs, five nouns, three places, six foods, etc.
2. It's possible to set a variety of tasks.

a)   Cut the verses up and get groups of students to put them in order. Cut individual lines up and do the same.

b)   Blank out some words and get students to fill them in (for the first listen don't give them the missing words. If they're struggling, present the missing words before the second listen).

c)   Replace some words with bogus ones, and challenge students to insert the correct word. For example: 'they're out to get you / there's zebras closing in on every side', or 'woke up this morning, smiled with the smiling sun / ten little ducks right on my doorstep'.

3. And of course, having studied the song, get students to sing it to end the lesson on a high note, so to speak.

Here is a list of songs that can be used in conjunction with particular types of grammar work.

Present Simple Tense

Our House – Madness (daily routines)

A Day in the Life (daily routines)

Wonderful Tonight (Third Person Sing)

Present Continuous

Complicated – Avril Lavigne

Don't Speak – No Doubt

Marlene on the Wall – Suzanne Vega
Live Forever - Oasis
Ob-la-di – The Beatles
Future Simple Tense – will
All My Loving – The Beatles
Past Simple Tense
America – Simon and Garfunkel
Are You Lonesome Tonight? – Elvis (+ Pres Simple Tense)
Used to be My Playground – Madonna (for 'used to')
Up The Junction - Squeeze
Present Perfect Tense
I Still Haven't Found… - U2
I Have Seen it All – Bjork
First Conditional
I'll Sail This Ship Alone – The Beautiful South
When I'm 64 – The Beatles
Second Conditional
Tears in Heaven – Eric Clapton
If I had a Million Dollars – Bare Naked Ladies
If I Were a Boy - Beyonce

Modals
It Must Be Love – Madness
Past Modals
Always on My Mind - Elvis
General
Zombie – The Cranberries
Thriller – Michael Jackson
Friday I'm in Love – The Cure (days of the week)
Angels – Robbie Williams

You're Beautiful – James Blunt

Goodbye My Lover – James Blunt

Candle in the Wind – Elton John (metaphor)

Do They Know It's Christmas? (discussion-based)

Manic Monday – The Bangles (routines)

Not Just a Pretty Face – Shania Twain (good for jobs)

Papa Don't Preach – Madonna

She – Elvis Costello

Zombie – The Cranberries (political)

Three Little Birds – Bob Marley

Why You Do the Things You Do – UB40 (adjectives)

Zebra – John Butler Trio (good for opposites)

Hand in My Pocket – Alanis Morissette (opposites)

Speaking

Of the four communication skills, speaking is arguably the most important (after all, you don't say 'she writes three languages,' do you?).

Students often enjoy speaking and experimenting with a new language, so it's important to provide opportunities for this. With speaking activities, the teacher's role is to give the students something to talk about, monitor what they're saying and help where necessary.

Clearly, when one student speaks the rest of the class is only listening. So with speaking activities it's far better to have students work in groups, so each student has more talk time. Once in groups, give students a specific task, or some form of competition, to give them a reason to talk. As with most lessons, give them a model to work with and the results will be better than simply saying 'ok, talk about food'. Here are a few ideas to get you going.

Picture Prompts

This is incredibly simple to arrange, and incredibly effective. The aim is simple: students are given a photograph and have one minute to talk about it. The image can be about almost anything – people, food, animals, science, nature – but make sure it has plenty of detail. The beauty of this exercise is that there is an element of pressure as students need to keep talking for a minute to complete the task and also that it works for students with a range of abilities. Elementary students can simply say what they see, the number of items, their colour or their shape. Higher-level students can say what they see but go beyond this, and give opinions and general statements about the image. For example, imagine we have a picture of five children swimming. The elementary student will say 'There are five children. They are swimming. There are two boys and three girls. The first boy has blue shorts.' And so on.

An intermediate student will say: 'I can see five children swimming, two boys and three girls. It looks like they are having fun. I like to swim at least once a week. Swimming is a great exercise because it helps you keep healthy'. And so on.

Conversation Poker

This is a great speaking activity that mimics a card game. Each student is given a short phrase, or function, that could be used as part of an everyday debate. All the functions are written on cards and dealt out to the players (groups of 4-5 work best). If a student can use the function in a natural and appropriate way, he or she puts the card in the middle. The first to get rid of all their cards is the winner.

The teacher needs to provide various topics to get the ball rolling, then listen to ensure students give appropriate answers, preferably with an extended answer. This activity works well as there is a strong element of competition that forces students to speak.

Here are some sample cards you could copy and use.

I think…	That's true but…
I don't think…	Yes, but…
What do you think about…?	Definitely!
How do you feel about…?	I don't agree.
I agree.	I also think…
I disagree.	What about…?
You're absolutely right!	On the whole, I agree with…
I'm sorry, I can't agree.	Yes, I think so too.
How about…?	Sorry but you're wrong!

Possible Topics

Chelsea are better than Manchester United.

Minecraft is the best video game.

Homework is a good idea.

Students should wear school uniform.

Italian food is the best in the world.

The internet is a good thing.

Role-play

Role-plays work well as students are able to take on a different persona, which tends to make them far less inhibited. Again, the idea of giving students a task – in this instance taking on a role – means they are thinking more about achieving the challenge and less about whether they are making mistakes.

Possible topics for this type of task are endless: newspaper stories, characters from books, a drama, a job interview, a television programme or interviewing a celebrity. Before letting the students loose, you'll need to warm the class up to whichever topic you've chosen. Use props, simple questions, anything that can spark interest.

Next, arrange the class in groups. Think about if you want one large group with lots of characters all playing a small part or whether it would be better to have smaller groups where each student has more opportunity to talk.

Alternatively, try 'hot-seating'. This is a technique where one student is selected to sit in a seat at the front of the class. Other students then think of questions to fire at their friend. For example, you could set up a murder-mystery scenario. There are five suspects and each has to be grilled by 'detectives' before the class decides who is guilty, and why. Or they could take on the role of a celebrity, preferably that's been involved in a recent scandal.

Teachers have their own roles to play here too. They should observe and let things flow, but jump in if students are truly stuck or going wildly off track. Other students should also be encouraged to listen and respond with opinions, to ensure they are not merely passive observers.

Taboo

Taboo is a simple game that is a guaranteed winner for any level. Students are given a card with four words on. They must describe the word at the top, but not use any of the other words to help them. For example, if the top word is 'London' the other words may be 'England, capital, Big Ben'. A student could therefore say 'This is a big city in the UK. Chelsea play football here.'

Put students in teams of at least three. Each person has a minute to describe as many words as possible. They cannot act, say 'the word rhymes with…' or say 'the first letter is…' The teacher needs to keep an eye on the speaker to ensure no 'taboo' words are mentioned. For low-level groups, simply get students to describe a word on a card, and don't worry about troublesome taboo words. Here are some examples you can copy and use, but make some of your own that fit with wherever you teach. Even better, get students to write their own cards. Taboo works well as students become so keen for their team to win that they forget they are learning.

20 questions

This is a classic parlour game that works just as well in the classroom. The rules are simple, the teacher thinks of something (person, food, place – it doesn't matter). Students then need to ask questions that only have a 'yes' or 'no' answer to discover what the answer is.

With lower-level students, begin by reviewing 'yes/no' questions: put simply, questions that start with an auxiliary verb (have/be/do) will usually produce a 'yes/no' response. Start with something simple (an apple) and work towards more obscure things that demand specific questions (a penguin). Once students establish an item is an animal, for example, they will tend to start simply yelling out the names of creatures so you'll need to encourage them to ask better questions (Can it fly? Has it got four legs? Does it live in Africa?)

Debates

Debating teams are an old favourite of schools, but with ESL classes you need to lay some ground rules, and provide lots of support. Debates can be used at almost any level, but the trick is finding something that students want to talk about and ensuring that they have sufficient vocabulary.

Firstly, make sure you have enough time to plan a debate. Pick a topic all students will be engaged with, probably something related to their own lives. Explain the basic structure of a debate: opening statements, presentations, questioning the other side, closing arguments. You'll then need to ensure students know some basic phrases for agreeing, disagreeing and giving opinions. Some of the functions below should help.

Functions

Functions are groups of words that do a specific job, such as helping you make a suggestion, offer advice or give a warning. Here are some of the main ones. Encourage students to think of the whole function, not individual words. Here are some of the most common.

Giving opinions

I think you should ....

You ought to ....

You should ....

If I were you, I'd ....

You'd better ....

Agreeing

I couldn't agree more

I (quite) agree.

I think you're absolutely right.

That's a very good point.

I totally agree.

Exactly!

Apologising

I'm sorry.

I apologise.

I'm sorry to say that ….

There seems to have been a mistake.

I beg your pardon.

Asking for more information

Sorry, but I'm not quite clear on…

I'd like to ask you about…

I'm not sure what you mean.

Could you explain that again, please?

What did you mean when you said .?

Could you give an example of .?

Asking for information

Excuse me.

Could you tell me …?

Could you tell me how to …?

Would you mind telling me …?

Do you know …?

What happens if …?

Where can I …?

When can I …?

How can I …?

Asking for opinions
What do you think about …?

What are you views on ...?

What do you feel about ...?

Do you have any particular views on ...?

Jigsaw conversations

Find an old train timetable, menu or tourism brochure. Make sure you have at least two copies then blank out different types of information on each one. Students are arranged in pairs and need to ask each other questions to complete their own document. Ensure that students are seated so that they cannot see each other's leaflet or menu.

This task works well as it uses real-life information and involves a challenge that requires students to speak in order to complete it.

CHAPTER 11: CULTURE CLASH

Survival Tips

Some people love change. Some people relish a challenge. Some people thrive on diversity. If you're any of those folk, then you're going to love life abroad.

If you hanker for a KFC every day and can't get your head around why they just don't do things like they do back home, then there could be trouble ahead.

Learning how to teach English is one thing; learning how to adapt to foreign cultures is something altogether different. You can master the Present Simple Tense in an afternoon but it can take years to come to terms with some aspects of living away from home.

Of course, the people you'll be working for may come from this alien culture, so you're going to need to get used to a different set of conditions. With that in mind, these are the top five essentials for life abroad:

1 Never, ever start a sentence 'but back home…' If life is that great back home, there's the door.

2 Smile. Even though the head of department has just asked you to work on Saturday when it's 4.30pm on Friday. Keeping cool goes a long way. It doesn't mean you have to give in to every demand, but you'll have a stronger argument if you aren't yelling. Many cultures, particularly Asian ones, are far less confrontational than those in the West.

3 Things go wrong. That's life, face it. The photocopier in your old office never worked that well either, so don't be amazed when the one in the staffroom starts smoking.

4 Things don't make sense. You may come from a place where logic is king and everything is done for a reason. You may think that such reasoning is absent from your school and the head of department lives in a fairy world where pixie dust falls from the sky and is transformed into students who can then magically speak English. Logic still exists here, it's just that it may not be the logic you're used to.

5 You're replaceable. Schools want people who fit in, work hard and are easy to work with. The one advantage you have is that the world of ESL has more than its fair share of people who struggle to achieve any of these, so if you keep your nose clean and your lesson plans complete, you'll be fine.

Expect the unexpected

Staffrooms vary from school to school and from country to country. Some local teachers will go out of their way to show you around; others may barely acknowledge your existence.

Sometimes everything can seem a mystery. During my first weeks as a teacher I shared a staff room with Thai workers, who did their best to speak some English from time to time, but generally conversations didn't extend much beyond 'good morning'. One afternoon I looked at my schedule and noticed two extra classes had been added on Mondays and Tuesdays. My assistant explained these were lessons about tourism, and that I didn't have to do much. That was understating things a little; it turned out I didn't have to do anything. The first lesson consisted of some children reading out a little English, and then my assistant took control and spoke Thai for the remainder of the class. After 15 minutes of standing at the front expecting to be called upon, I took a moment to enquire exactly what I should be doing.

'Oh, in this lesson you don't do anything, you can sit down if you like,' my assistant said.

'Maybe tomorrow I should bring a book,' I joked.

'Yes, good idea.'

For the remainder of the lesson, and subsequent ones, I was no more than a bystander. And if they happened to have lessons outside and it was a bit hot, I could skip those and stay in the nice air-conditioned staff room. The school hadn't allocated me as many lessons as local teachers, so they tagged these ones on so at least it appeared I was doing the same amount of work.

In addition to phantom classes, you may well come across the request for an 'urgent' meeting that transpires to be as crucial as having enough teabags for the staffroom. Before my second day at school I was told to get in by 7.30am, 20 minutes earlier than normal. Keen to please, I was there at 7.15am and waited as 7.30am passed, and then 7.45am came and went, and finally assembly began and there seemed to be no good reason for my early arrival. The only reassuring thing was that everyone else seemed to have a purpose and know what was going on, and I felt confident that eventually they would think to let me in on the secret. Sometimes it's better, no actually essential, to go with the flow and stop asking questions.

How to not put your foot in it – or on it

Going abroad isn't the same as living abroad. If you're on a two-week break to Hanoi, nobody expects you to completely embrace Vietnamese culture. When you start renting a house and going to an office every day, things change.

You've decided to live in a foreign country, so you need to understand what they do and why they do it. Most countries have their little quirks and superstitions. Learning what they are not only ensures you don't cause offence; it can always enhance your experience in that country.

Take Thailand, for example. A country many assume is full of easy-going, relaxed folk. And for the most part it is, but get things wrong and you can set them off worse than a bottle of Coke that's just rolled down a hill. Two things are of utmost importance in Thailand – the Monarchy and the family. Never, ever think of saying anything derogatory about either of these.

The Thai King, Bhumibol Adulyadej, was the world's longest-reigning monarch, having ascended to the throne in 1946. Strict lese majeste rules prevent any criticism of the Royal family. Times may be changing, but even subtle barbs can land you with a major problem. A drunken Swiss man in Chiang Mai was once jailed for ten years after spray-painting posters of the King. He was later pardoned.

Another great way to cause offence in many Asian cultures is with your feet and head. The head is the highest part of the body, both literally and spiritually. Conversely, the feet are the lowest part. A person's head is off-limits and is never touched. When getting past someone who is seated, the person going by will bow to effectively apologise for having his or her head at a higher level.

At the other end, feet are considered the basest part of the body and are never used to point. Thais will not step over somebody who is lying down and the soles of the feet never point directly at someone.

Getting it wrong can have serious consequences. A newly-arrived tourist in Phuket once ordered a drink in a bar. As he pulled out some coins a few fell to the floor and he stopped them rolling away by putting his feet on them. A group of nearby Thais saw the man's foot stamp on the coins – which bear an image of the King's face – and was so enraged he was set upon.

Whatever you do, in any culture, never blow your top. Think about your actions and what may have gone wrong. Most people are forgiving of those from other cultures, so a little humility always helps.

In other countries, holding up your hand with your forefinger and thumb touching in an 'OK' sign can be extremely offensive, while declining gifts of food and drink can also be perceived as a sign of ill-breeding. Here are a few others to bear in mind:

- In the US, it's common to beckon someone with a finger, but in other cultures this is how you'd address an animal and won't win many friends.
- In the Middle East and most of Asia, the left hand is used for bathroom functions and so is not used to touch people or food.
- Touching a child on the head may seem like a sign of affection, but in Buddhist countries this is taboo.
- You may well want to take pictures of certain native groups you come across. Ask first though, as some believe the image you take will also include a part of their spirit.
- Hispanic and Asian cultures don't always like making eye contact. Don't take this as a sign that they're not listening or attentive.

Perhaps the best way to get a grip with other cultures is to offer some brief stories about some of the things that make life abroad so fascinating, and challenging.

Anecdotes

- One Science Day consisted of dozens of tables showing everything from a baby great white shark in a pickle jar and a dissected frog to an array of microscopes with the banner 'where do I come from?' above each one.

There was no teaching and so I wandered about some of the stalls. I approached one display and peered at photographs of a couple of tiny atoms, when a 12-year-old girl looked up from her table and asked: 'Would you like to look at some sperm?'

This just seemed wrong on so many levels. A flurry of lines went in and out of my head and I opted to just smile and thank her for the offer, while peering at the sperm which were jiggling about merrily in their Petri dish. I thought it best not to enquire where she obtained the sample.

- During a discussion on pastimes, I asked my co-teacher to bring in some of her interests, and she produced Bad Boys II and a Bruce Willis flick. Things were going well, and I tried a few questions out on the class

'What does Miss Tai do in her spare time?'

'She does Bad Boys', one student said, innocently. I frowned at him but figured no-one else got it so rapidly moved on.

- During a tourism lesson, my only task for two hours was to read some text to the class. The problem with this was that it featured a string of place names. I gamely attempted a few of these and thought my efforts were reasonable, until I came to Nong Yai. A few of the students tittered at my pronunciation, which I assumed meant I'd hit the wrong inflection, but when it cropped up again, even more laughed. By this point it seemed clear their new teacher had something inappropriate, and my co-teacher wasn't about to translate. It was left for a friend to later tell me that Nong Yai is slang for 'enormous vagina.

- Remember what we said about choosing the right material? That didn't quite happen during one reading exercise my co-teacher had produced. She gave out a worksheet about the Thai beach resort of Pattaya, famed for its 30,000-plus bar girls and exotic/erotic nightlife. The sheet boldly informed the 13-year-olds: 'You will find a profusion of clubs and cabarets which cater to every taste and persuasion, and Pattaya's famously charming hostesses will delight all your senses.' I bet they couldn't wait for the field trip. Still, it wasn't as bad as the teacher who got sacked from an all-girls Catholic school for

- doing a lesson on the merits of birth control.
- Activities can take precedence over lessons, especially when the school is asking parents to pay for a show their children are performing in. Academic camps are also a big deal, although they don't tend to be academic and there usually isn't any actual camping involved. I was measured up for a special T-shirt (which didn't arrive in time) and asked to come up with a game for the students to keep them amused for an hour.

My plan was for students to bring in a local English-language newspaper, pick out 20 words and then translate them. If there was time, they were to then use the words in a new sentence.

In the afternoon one group was lagging and had done very little for the first 20 minutes. As soon as I went over to check on them it became obvious why.

They had brought along a copy of the German version of the local newspaper. Even when I patiently explained their mistake a couple of them carried on searching for words they didn't know – which amounted to all of them – before I removed the paper and added the word 'muppet' to their vocabulary.

- During a visit to a school for some speaking tests, I was led up a flight of stairs to the classrooms. At the top of the stairs a large, beautifully-design mural had been stuck to the wall. And in giant, cut-out letters the word 'cock' was staring at me.

I looked again and saw that alongside other signs said: 'badgers', 'elephants', 'foxes'. The Irish teacher leading the way nodded apologetically and said 'I know, we told them, we told them…'

- At another speaking test in a different school everything had gone smoothly and we had spent the morning testing students and a few teachers. Students, it turned out, were far easier to deal with. Usually the tests are done in pairs, with a group of three at the end if there is an odd number of candidates. At this school there was indeed an odd number of teachers, but rather than be given a group of three, they remained in pairs and the last teacher came in with a woman who had done the test 10 minutes earlier.

Pointing this out to the co-ordinator, I was told the last candidate didn't get on with those she was meant to be in a group of three with. The solution was to get the other woman to do the whole test again to make up the numbers. A great example of when it's best to simply nod and accept that this is how it is.

- At one secondary school all the female students were lined up for assembly. Teachers then went along the ranks to check if the girls were wearing bras - by feeling their shirts. Bras were not deemed appropriate for 16-year-old girls and the school preferred them to wear plaited hair and long skirts that resembled parachutes.
- Another teacher, an American named John, took great pleasure in lining 20 children up and setting them in a semi-press up stance. He then proceeded to yell at them in the middle of the assembly area, watched by 100 curious kids, while he made them sing the alphabet. All very humiliating, and all of which had the required effect. A while later we were told to refrain from any 'unusual' punishments. Cracking a metal ruler over their knuckles was fine, but let's not take the piss out of them, please.
- At the start of a new school year we were shown to a new staff room. All of the carefully-cataloged materials from our erstwhile office now lay scattered over a classroom floor.

In our new staff room the one thing that had been neatly stacked was a collection of glossy hard-back books. Still in their plastic covers, we started to unwrap them to see what educational treasures we'd been given.

Among the books were 'Later Italian Paintings in the National

Gallery of Ireland', 'Scottish Lighthouses', New Austrian Architecture', 'Turf Grass: Science and Management' and a tome about great fireplaces of our time. Given that this sub-tropical nation wasn't particularly in need of fireplaces, great or otherwise, and that new Austrian architecture is possibly even less gripping than the old style, you have to wonder just what someone was thinking. To this day, they remain in their covers, untouched by ESL hands.

- At a teachers' dinner one of the school bosses walked around to greet new teachers. When he reached one of the recruits, he tried to make small talk by asking where he was from.

'Pakistan', said the teacher.

'Ah, welcome. You're not in the Taliban are you?' came the instant reply. Oh, how we laughed. Nervously.

- When teaching, there are several words to avoid as they simply cause more trouble than they're worth. If you teach in Thailand, within your first week of teaching you'll almost certainly hear students talking about flying kites, as this is the Thai slang for masturbation (thanks to similar hand movements).

The word 'judo' caused one class to fall apart in tears of merriment and nothing I did could get them back again. Turns out that 'judo' happens to sound exactly the same as 'erect penis' in Thai. Oh, and be wary of calling anything 'fun', as that's slang for sex.

CHAPTER 12: ASSESSMENTS

Types of Tests

Checking that students actually understand what you're teaching them is an important part of the job. There are all kinds of ways to do this (speaking tests, project work), but the overwhelming favourite is by written exam.

Schools like such exams as they're simple to mark and it's easy to then grade students. Tests rarely give you a completely accurate guide of what a student can do, but they're not a bad benchmark. Remember that just because a student scores high or low, they aren't necessarily good or bad at English. Some students prefer the tension of an exam (and knowing you're facing one does tend to lead to more revision), while others may be able to communicate well but freeze when faced with an academic test. Either way, sooner or later (probably sooner) you'll be asked to write such a test.

There are several 'musts' when it comes to creating an exam. Firstly, only test students on what they are expected to know. A school once gave students an English test showing Big Ben, the White House, the Statue of Liberty and the Pyramids. The question asked which one of these was in Egypt. Now that would be great for a general knowledge test, but it doesn't actually test the students' English ability.

Secondly, think about what kind of questions you want. Some formats are easy to produce but don't fully test students, while others are tricky to make but simple to mark.

Thirdly, bear in mind how long the test will last. If you create the perfect 200-question exam but only give students 30 minutes to complete it, you're not going to get a true picture of what your class can do. Similarly, if your test includes a large text that needs to be read, that's going to eat up a considerable amount of time too. For exams, it's better to have several easy-to-digest chunks of comprehension texts rather than one long one.

Lastly, consider how you're going to mark the test. If there are open questions, then you'll need to come up with some marking scheme. Or if some questions are far easier or less complex than others, you may need to weight the marks.

These are the main ways of testing students (if you want to impress your boss, refer to them as elicitation techniques).

- **Multiple choice questions**

These are popular as they are easy to mark, something worth considering if you have 500 or so students to test. Multiple-choice tests sound simple enough, but you need to be sure there is only one possible answer. It's also worth checking that you haven't made the question too complex for the students' level, as then you'll largely be testing their reading skills, which isn't what you'd planned on. They aren't perfect; you are effectively giving the answer rather than seeing if students can come up with but they are popular.

Example 1: A person who flies a plane is called

a) a banker   b) a teacher   c) a pilot   d) a doctor

Example 2: They _____ playing tennis at the moment.

a) is   b) are   c) am   d) was

- **Gap-fill** Similar to multiple-choice but without any options. It's easy to make and the only real obstacle is being aware of more than one possible answer. Students shouldn't miss out on a point just because they've come up with an answer you hadn't anticipated. This is a good way to check tenses as, if you're feeling generous, you can give the base form of the verb in brackets as a clue. If there's only one possible answer, try to leave it out.

Example 1: Yesterday, James _____ a new car (buy)

Example 2: He _____ gone to Bangkok.

- **Matching** Students are given two groups of words or sentences and have to put them together. This could be a simple vocabulary test (apple/banana, cow/pig) or it could be used for far more complex patterns.

Example:

a) She is interested   1) of spiders

b) Gary is frightened   2) in the supernatural

- **Transformation** You give students a sentence and they then have to change it based on given instructions. It's a good way of testing grammar, but just because a student can make the structure, it doesn't mean they understand what it means.

Example 1: Is the giraffe on the left or right _____ (tall, comparative)?

Example 2: If it's sunny at the weekend I _____ the park (First Conditional)

- **Comprehension questions/true or false** After a reading passage or listening exercise, students can be asked a series of questions to check their understanding. Think about whether you want closed questions that are simple to mark or ones that invite a more open answer, which will take longer to mark but undoubtedly tell you more about what the student knows. With a little effort you can transform these into true or false questions.

Example: *'Barack Obama was born in Hawaii. His father was from*

Kenya and his mother was a white American from Kansas. His mother divorced and married Lolo Soetoro, from Indonesia. Barack went to school in Indonesia until he was ten years old. Then he went back to Hawaii.'

Comprehension question: Where was Obama's father from?
_____

True/False question: Obama's father was born in Indonesia. T/F

There are several other ways to test, such as dictation (the teacher reads a passage and students write it down), essays or speaking tests. Try to mix these up so students are used to a range of exams.

Tests don't have to just be the thing students do at the end of term. They can be given at the end of each unit to check progress and they should include listening and speaking elements where possible.

Have a look at these questions and see if you can tell which, if any, could be problematic.

Questions

1 (gap-fill)

I _____ tennis.

2 (multiple choice)

There _____ two pens on the table.

a) are   b) isn't   c) aren't   d) won't

3 (multiple choice)

Buckingham Palace is in _____.

a) Manchester   b) London   c) Amsterdam   d) New York

4 (open questions) Write a 100-word postcard to your friend about your last holiday.

Answers

1 The options are too great. Possible answers include 'hate', 'love', 'enjoy', 'like', 'loathe'. If you set this question be clear that any grammatically correct answer is acceptable.

2 Unless your students can see the table in question, they won't know if 'are' or 'aren't' are correct. There should only be one possible answer with this kind of question. Think logically as well as grammatically.

3 If you're testing students on general knowledge, then fine. If not, this question doesn't work. A student may well understand the question but their knowledge of London landmarks may not be up to scratch.

4 To be honest, this question is fine. The problem comes when you and your colleagues are marking it. To get full marks will the student have to write perfectly or are you judging them based on what they should be able to do at this point in time? If a student uses the present tense, not the past, to describe their last holiday, how heavily do you penalise him/her?

Giving the Test

You'd be amazed at how cunning and sneaky students can be when it comes to cheating in a test. Assume that any student will take a peek at a friend's answers given half a chance. To prevent this, always make sure there is a teacher in the room. And always make sure that said teacher is actively observing the exam, not fiddling with their phone.

If the test is in a classroom, think about the classroom layout. Moving desks is preferable but if that can't be done, place the students' school bags or some object between students so subtle glances to a neighbouring answer sheet are more tricky.

Try and ensure all students are tested at the same time, if they aren't then mobile phones are a great way to pass on answers. And lastly, save your test as you can use it again next year, just change some of the questions around.

CHAPTER 13: WHERE TO TEACH?

OK, so you have your TEFL certificate, you know what a gerund is and you can write a lesson plan with your eyes closed. The next thing is to think about where you want to teach.

ESL Hotspots

If you want to look elsewhere for work, other Asian countries offer a huge variety of work options. Some are more challenging than others, but all are looking for ESL teachers. Here are some basic tips about the main ESL hotspots.

Australia: The once thriving ESL industry in Australia has diminished of late, thanks largely to new visa regulations and the rise of the Aussie dollar. Expect to have some competition if you got for an ESL position here.

As for language schools, many tend to be multicultural, especially those in Sydney. One class could easily be made up of 7 or more different nationalities. Expect to meet students that are Thai, Chinese, Korean, South American, European, Japanese, Vietnamese, Indian and Egyptian. Their ages range from 18-60 but the majority are 20-25 year olds either on holiday, there to work (but couldn't get a working visa) or those who have come out specifically to improve their English in an English-speaking country.

Student turnover can be anything from 1-2 weeks to 6-12

months, so the class dynamic is always likely to be changing. Many schools rotate a library of 3-4 text books to avoid repetition for those students who stay on but don't make much progress within their level. General English courses are on the slide – that used to be mainly for study/holiday trips - and IELTS is increasingly popular. This is because universities have raised their IELTS's entry levels for most courses and in order to apply for permanent residency. For residency, a band 5 gets you 15 points while a 6 results in 20 points, the same as native speakers. International students must study at least 20 hours per week in order to fulfill their visa regulations. Classes tend to run for four hours a day.

Websites

www.ueca.edu.au - University English Centres Australia

www.englishaustralia.com.au

Cambodia: Few private schools means pickings are limited here. Phnom Penh is your main chance of landing a decent job, but don't expect to retire on your earnings. A handful of international schools operate around the main cities, and these will definitely require ESL teachers, but usually ones that are fully qualified. Elsewhere, teaching Business English to adults is an option.

China: Plenty of teaching opportunities in China, as more people learn English here than anywhere else in the world. Those wanting to teach in China will find things much easier if they have a degree and teaching experience, though curiously a TEFL certificate is not always essential. Most foreigners work in Beijing or Shanghai, although there are also opportunities to work in more remote areas; indeed, it will probably be easier to pick up work in the more unusual locations. Schools or institutions want their pound of flesh from foreign teachers, so be clear if you want weekends to yourself or are only willing to work certain hours. Being China, some subjects (namely, politics) are off limits in the classroom and students can be notoriously difficult to elicit responses from, but there are a growing number of learners who see the importance of mastering English, and are committed to doing so.

Websites

http://www.teachabroadchina.com/

Japan: Good money, dedicated students and great facilities make this a popular choice. Schools can be choosy over who they hire and a degree plus experience are usually preferred, however there are some pickings for those without either. The cost of living can be high if you stay around the major cities.

While there are many opportunities in schools and businesses for ESL teachers, the most attractive option is known as the Jet programme. Salaries are higher, conditions are better – but the queue to get accepted is far longer.

Students are generally well-behaved and well-motivated, but more modern learners may need a little motivation and may occasionally be unruly. Sitting and filling in endless gap-fill sentences isn't enough and more dynamic lessons will be handy. Living in Japan can be a fascinating experience, although non-Caucasian looking teachers may unfortunately find some barriers in their way.

Websites

www.jetprogramme.org

Middle East: If you can put up with a lack of alcohol, limited nightlife and desert-like conditions, many Middle Eastern countries offer superb salaries and conditions. Business English jobs are especially sought-after here, but you'll need to be qualified to the hilt and have at least 3 years' experience.

Websites

www.teachmideast.com

Philippines: Given the diverse nature of this island nation, there is also a great range of work. Living standards are generally lower than in other Southeast Asian countries, which is partly why so many Filipinos choose to work abroad. Salaries are also low (a qualified local teacher may only receive $200 a month) but if you chose the right island it can be a great experience.

Students themselves are generally open to learning and, compared to other Southeast Asian countries, are confident about using English. It is a requirement for students to pass English or else face remaining stuck at the same level – so there is a huge incentive to pass tests, which means motivation is rarely lacking.

Living in the Philippines is easy as English is an official language and is widely spoken. Children begin learning English in kindergarten and this continues through to university. While native English speakers are not generally found in mainstream classrooms, there is work at international and private schools. You may also see jobs at universities being offered, but the pay there is usually low. For an ESL teacher, private work may be the easiest way to secure a reasonable income.

South America: If you can speak Spanish, you may well be on to a winner here. South America is a diverse, complex continent with plenty of opportunities for ESL teachers who fancy an adventure. Take Chile, for example. The capital, Santiago, is surrounded by the mighty Andes and also happens to be a rather developed, got-its-act-together kind of city filled with fine restaurants and museums. On the downside, time-keeping isn't considered particularly important. If you have a TEFL certificate, you are in with a good shout of landing a job. Most teachers work in private institutes or universities. Look closely before you sign up, as standards and resources vary wildly. You may find it hard to get work before you get in the country, so don't give up if nobody replies to your emails.

Or there is Colombia. The overall standard of English here is low, so even in university classes you'll be aiming your classes at pre-intermediate level. This lack of English skills means there is a corresponding demand for teachers who can help locals get better. Forget all those headlines that tell of kidnapping and drug cartels; nearly all of Colombia is accessible and its people friendly.

Over in Uruguay, teaching jobs can be found in private schools, where classes of around ten are the norm. Adults come to learn English after work and are a friendly and chatty crowd. To say you won't get rich in Uruguay is an absurd understatement, but your hourly rate will still be more than enough to get by and still allow you to get out and explore the country. Apartments with sea views can be found for $500 a month, so you may want to take a few savings with you. Plus points are stunning architecture, a Mediterranean lifestyle and good weather. On the downside the only food worth getting excited about is steak. Quality bottles of wine cost as much as a soft drink does back home.

Websites

www.southamerica.cl

South Korea: Jobs here tend to pay well and the cost of living isn't as high as you may think, making it a good place to spend a year if you want to get some savings. Koreans are notoriously studious students, and often will have their heads in books until late at night. The push for more Koreans to learn English is huge – students need to pass a basic test to enter universities – and this means many private institutions offer courses. Where you attend university will have a huge influence on the rest of your life and, consequently high school is one tough place. Students regularly study from 7am-10pm and even private lessons after this to top things off. Studying until 3am is quite common; one Korean says (with no trace of irony) that those who can sleep four hours a night will reap the benefits later in life. Not surprisingly, the resultant pressure can have devastating effects: students who can't match up to such towering expectations sometimes commit suicide.

There are three basic levels of education in Korea:

1) 'Hagwons', or language institutes, can be a mixed bag so it's wise to get several opinions before signing up with one. Those which have been in business longer may well tend to be the better ones. The hagwon is a private school which crams students for after-school, or even pre-school, classes. Conditions can be challenging: expect shift work from 6am-10am then 7pm-11pm with five or ten days holiday a year for the lowest salaries.

Teachers regularly get cheated out of their contractual benefits, such as severance pay and return flights. Taking on such institutions is an expensive and largely unproductive exercise. As a result, these hagwons tend to be filled with under-qualified folk who would struggle to get jobs in Burger King back home. If you are qualified (a degree and a TEFL), you should be able to do better.

2) EPIK is Korea's biggest employer of foreigners in education. Be sure to check out their standard contract online at www.epik.go.kr. EPIK recruits all the teachers for public primary and secondary schools in South Korea. Most jobs offer a competitive salary, housing and, crucially, a stepping stone to the more lucrative university gigs.

Conditions have become slightly less generous in recent years (the four months annual leave has been slashed to ten days) and some places may force you to go in even when the students are at home. It's euphemistically known as 'desk warming'. Find a level-headed teacher though and you may be able to stay home like the students. Level-headed teachers can be surprisingly thin on the ground though, so don't expect logic and reason to win many arguments.

3) University jobs. Now we're talking. These are the Holy Grail for every expat in Korea. Put simply: you get paid a lot to do very little. Think 12 hours a week, no requirement to sit in an office for no clear reason, and at least one day a week off. After your first semester, you could even insist on that free day being a Monday or Friday, or even both if you're feeling confident. You could also ask to just teach mornings or afternoons. Should you get bored by the lack of work, you can do overtime, for which you will be generously reimbursed. Still not convinced? Then throw in two major vacations a year, each lasting 11 weeks, one in the winter and one in the summer. Most unis tend to stick to these conditions but, inevitably, there are some that don't so you'll need to do your own homework before signing up with one. As these are the plum jobs, universities can be picky about who they want. Nevertheless, after a couple of years of teaching and a little luck, you could certainly start applying.

Thailand

Thailand is a hugely varied kingdom, and teaching in Bangkok is very different from teaching upcountry. Take some time to consider how close to Bangkok you want to be, whether you want beaches at the weekends and if you're going to crave Western food now and again.

With 10 million people, Bangkok is the place to be if you want some action. World-class restaurants, the best nightlife by a neon-light year and a good number of English-speaking locals make Bangkok a vibrant place to be. It's also the most expensive spot, and you'll need a salary of 40,000 baht a month (US $1,300) or more to enjoy it. The range of schools is vast, from government institutions up to the best international schools, which pay teachers more than they would get in their homeland. Bangkok can be ridiculously busy and slow-moving, but it's also filled with the most culture, entertainment – and other foreigners – than anywhere else in Thailand.

In the area known as the Eastern Seaboard, which includes the provinces of Chonburi and Rayong, there are nearly as many beaches as there are schools. It's also an hour or so from Bangkok, making it a popular place to work.

To see what most of Thailand is really like, you need to go upcountry. Teach in the north or northeast and you may well be kissing goodbye to life's luxuries. With some exceptions, notably Korat in the northeast and Chiang Mai and Chiang Rai in the north, most towns here are simple affairs where you can get a real feel for Thai life. Chiang Mai is a historic city with a relatively compact feel to it and a growing expat scene, while Korat has fewer features but is the northeast's largest city. Things will be cheap, but your salary may not top 30,000 baht. Expect to be slurping noodles most evenings while swapping stories with the town's expats.

Vietnam: One of Southeast Asia's most developing countries, Vietnam has several locations that are great places to live and teach. As well as the two main cities of the northern capital Hanoi and the southern Ho Chi Minh City, there are long stretches of coastline filled with fine beaches and countryside area filled with patchwork rice fields. To teach, you'll need a degree and, preferably, a TEFL certificate. Most work centres on universities, as many young Vietnamese are very keen on honing their English skills. Private teaching can also provide a good income.

Western countries: Given the influx of immigrants in many nations, there is always high demand for ESL teachers. Don't discount getting some experience teaching at home first; it will look good on your CV and give you extra confidence when you start working abroad. See the next chapter for links to websites that offer detailed advice and job vacancies.

CHAPTER 14: WEBSITES AND RESOURCES

Years ago, teachers would have to sit down with a blank piece of paper and map out a lesson from scratch. There was no place to go for inspiration, no vast resources to draw on, no quick fix.

Today, thanks to the internet, there is a lesson for every occasion. Not only that, there are plenty of forums so when Somchai falls asleep for the third lesson in a row, you have somewhere to offload your angst.

Most schools will have internet access; some may even have interactive whiteboards in the classroom where you can display your online dexterity.

Below are some of the top websites for ESL teachers.

Jobs

www.ajarn.com – the grand-daddy of websites for teachers in Thailand, with vacancies, a lively forum and some informative features.

www.eflmagazine.com - book reviews, resources and regularly-updated blog posts.

www.eslbase.com – more generic site that offers jobs from around the world.

www.teflasia.com – good for the basics, but could do with more content.

www.tefl.com – the main international site for ESL folk with massive jobs database.

Teaching resources

www.abcteach.com – plenty of primary resources

www.bbc.co.uk/worldservice/learningenglish – excellent way of bringing news into your classroom.

www.breakingnewsenglish.com/index.html

www.britishcouncil.org - go to the teaching link for discussions and advice for teaching ESL.

www.cambridgesol.org/ - the place to find out about Cambridge's suite of exams

www.eflclub.com/ - simple site for more advanced students.

www.enchantedlearning.com – graphics-heavy site for younger learners.

www.englishbaby.com – free membership for students and great resources.

www.englishclub.com/ - well-designed site for students.

www.englishexercises.org – an activity for every grammar point around.

www.english-to-go.com – information-packed site, but a subscription is needed.

www.eslcafe.com – Dave's ESL café is arguably the best-established and best-run ESL site around.

http://eslkidsworld.com – ideal place to pick up some printables.

www.esl-galaxy.com – tons of free material.

www.esl-lesson-plan.com – busy general site with plenty of resources

http://eslteachingideas.blogspot.com – ideas for music lessons and plenty more.

http://free-english-study.com – gorgeous site for self-study.

www.hospitalenglish.com – for when you're asked to teach nurses and doctors.

http://esligcse.webs.com – fantastic site for anyone taking IGCSE ESL.

http://iteslj.org/ - hundreds of games and activities.

www.learnenglish.com – busy site with podcasts and Q&A section for students.

www.learnenglish.de/ - excellent range of activities and topics.

www.linguarama.com/ps/index.html - perfect for teachers of Business English.

www.onestopenglish.com – huge collection of themed lesson plans. Subscription needed.

http://sitesforteachers.com – links to more than 1,000 teaching sites.

www.teachingenglish.org.uk – superb collection of resources, lesson plans and essays.

http://tefltunes.com – brilliant site for music-based ESL classes.

www.theteacherscorner.net/ - ideal if you need to teach more than just English.

http://waze.net/oea/ - dedicated to improving students' speaking skills.

Theory

Developingteachers.com – interesting articles about teaching.

CHAPTER 15: GLOSSARY OF ACRONYMS AND TERMS

The world of English language teaching is full of acronyms and technical terms. Some you can learn and then lock away in a dusty box and never look at again. Others you'll want to keep in your pocket and bring out on a regular basis.

Here are the main acronyms for ESL (see, we've started already) and also a helpful list of terminology.

A

Accent – differences based purely on pronunciation.

Active Skills – speaking and listening, as opposed to reading and writing.

Adjective – a word that describes a noun (the *black* bag).

Adverb – a word or phrase that describes a verb, adjective or another adverb, (he ran *quickly*. He *sometimes* plays tennis). They often, but not always, end in –ly.

Antonym - a word that has the opposite meaning to another (beautiful – ugly).

Articles – 'a/an' and 'the'. The definite article is 'the', the indefinite is 'a/an'.

Auxiliary verbs – verbs such as 'be', 'do' and 'have' that help form sentences, but play a lesser role than the main verb.

B

Behaviourism – a theory linked with B.F. Skinner that states if X occurs because of Y, the subject is likely to continue doing Y in anticipation of receiving X. When this happens, learning is said to have occurred. In teaching, the thinking goes that students respond to a stimulus, and this needs to be rewarded if it is to be repeated.

Business English – Teaching English to adults with a focus on practical skills, such as writing emails, interviews or justifying opinions.

C

Cambridge ESOL – The University of Cambridge is responsible for several graded English language examinations. The tests begin with YLE (Young Learner Examinations), made up of Starters, Movers and Flyers, and then progress to 5 upper levels: KET (Key English Test), PET (Preliminary English Test), FCE (First Certificate of English), CAE (Certificate of Advanced English) and CPE (Certificate of Proficiency in English).

Capital letters – use for Concrete nouns (Tom, London, River Seine)

CELTA – (See 'DELTA') Certificate in English Language Training for Adults. Considered one of the best training courses.

CLT (Communicative Language Teaching) A method that promotes the use of authentic materials and real-life situations.

Communicative competence – knowing what to say and when to say it.

Collocation – two words that commonly are used together (utter failure, complete success).

Complex Sentences – sentences with two or more main clauses.

Conditionals – 'if' plus a condition. There are four conditional clauses in English. Zero Conditional (If you touch hot water, you burn your hands), First Conditional: If it is sunny, we will go to the beach), Second Conditional: If I had enough money, I would buy a new car and Third Conditional (If I had known you were coming, I would have bought cakes).

Conjunctions - a word that links sentences or clauses (so, because, and).

Creole – when a pidgin language becomes the first language.

D

DELTA – Diploma in English Language Training for Adults.

Demonstratives – words that can be determiners or pronouns and can be singular or plural (this, that, these, those).

Determiners – (also known as articles) Usually 'a/an' and 'the' but can also talk about possession (his) and quantity (few).

Dialect – differences based on geographic location. Also considers syntax and vocabulary.

Diphthongs – vowels that glide from one sound to the next (boat).

Drill – a speaking activity where the students simply repeat the teacher's words.

E

EAL – English as an Additional Language.

EFL – English as a Foreign Language.

ELT – English Language Training.

ESA – Engage, Study, Activate: an established three-step teaching method that introduces a topic or idea, allows students to study it and establish any rules, and ends with students using the topic or idea.

ESL – English as a Second Language.

ESP – English for Special Purposes, such as business English.

F

Functions – parts of language used for a specific purpose, such as arguing, asking, or agreeing.

G

Gap-fill – a popular exercise for course books where students fill in the blanks.

Gerund – the –ing form of a verb when used as a noun (*smoking* is bad for you). Pronounced 'je-rund', not 'ga-rund'.

H

HOD – Head of Department.

Homonym – a word that has the same sound and spelling as another but has a different meaning (ball – the round thing you kick, ball – a formal dance).

Homophone – a word that has the same sound but different spelling from another word (right/write, air/heir).

I

IELTS – International English Language Testing System.

International Phonetic Alphabet – a standard alphabet for phonemes.

Intonation – the part of pronunciation that expresses emotion, or questions or understanding.

Irregular verbs – Past Tense or Past Participle verbs that do not end with –ed (went, thought, saw)

J

Jigsaw – a group or pair activity where one student receives limited information and must communicate with another student to find all the answers.

Journals – teachers are often asked to complete journals, a reflective log about how their lessons went.

L

L1 – a student's native language.

L2 – the language a student learns.

Levels – students are usually split into groups according to ability. Levels go from starter – elementary – pre-intermediate – intermediate – upper-intermediate – advanced.

Lexical – the vocabulary of a language.

Linguistics – the study of language. It includes phonology (how a sound is made), phonology (sound patterns), syntax (linking sounds and patterns) and semantics (meaning).

M

Metaphor – a literary term to say one thing literally is another.

Minimal Pairs – words that have only one different phoneme (buy/sigh, see/tea).

Modal Verbs – special verbs that deal with asking, ordering or giving advice (should, must, have to, can).

Model – the ideal use of language, given by teachers as an example for students.

N

Nouns – things, places or people (Bob, Egypt, idea).

O

Object – part of a sentence that 'receives' the verb (they ate *pizza*).

OHP – overhead projector.

OHT – overhead transparency.

Onomatopoeia – words that sound like their meaning (crash, whisper, soft, buzz).

P

Passive Skills – listening and reading, as opposed to writing and speaking.

Passive Voice – a sentence which is not interested in saying who does an action. The Passive Voice is used when we want to put a different importance to the object or subject (Toyota cars *are made* by the Japanese).

Pedagogy – the science of teaching.

Phoneme – the smallest part of sound in English. Phonemes have their own alphabet to describe all possible sounds in the English language.

Phonetics – the study of how sound is made.

Phonology – the study of sound patterns.

Pidgin English – (see also Creole) a system of language that helps people with no common tongue.

PGCE – Post Graduate Certificate of Education: The standard qualification used for teachers in the United Kingdom. This or the equivalent is usually required to work as a mainstream teacher in international schools.

PPP – Presentation, Practice, Production: An established teaching method, ideal for lower-level groups.

Prepositions – words that can describe time, movement, or place (*at* 3pm, *into* the house, *on* top).

Pronouns – words that replace nouns in a sentence. There are different kinds: subject pronouns – 'I, you they'; object pronouns – he, me, them; reflexives – 'myself'; possessive – 'mine, ours'; relative – 'who, whose, which, that and where'.

Punctuation – the forgotten figure of English language teaching. Some languages have vastly different punctuation rules, so it is something students need to study. Many Asian languages have no full stops or capital letters, so these are areas where some students can trip up.

R

Received Pronunciation (RP) – what used to be a recognised standard of 'correct' pronunciation. Imagine a BBC presenter from the 1950s.

Register – different styles depending on levels of formality and themes. For example, a person would talk differently to the Queen than with their friend in the pub.

Regular verbs – past tense verbs that end –ed (looked)

S

Schwa – the most common sound in English. The final syllable of 'better' has a schwa. In phonetics, it is represented as a reversed 'e'.

Semantics – deals with the meaning of words.

Simile – comparing two things that are not similar. Similes use 'as' or 'like' (the car coughed like an old smoker).

Stylistics – a linguistic look at literary language. Stylistics may analyse poetry, newspapers or novels.

Synonym – a word with a similar or identical meaning to another.

Syntax – links sounds patterns and meaning.

T

TBL (Task-Based Learning) – activities where students learn by accomplishing a challenge, rather than focus specifically on English. Examples may include completing a train timetable or discussing what five items a group would need on a desert island.

TEFL – Teaching English as a Foreign Language. Used where English is not the main language in a country.

TESL – Teaching English as a Second Language. This may seem identical to TEFL, but it refers to teaching English alongside the native language, for example in India.

TESOL – Teaching English to Speakers of Other Languages.

Timelines – useful for describing tenses.

TOEIC – Test of English for International Communication. Tests that focus on Business English.

TTT – Teacher Talking Time – the amount of time a teacher spends addressing a class. This should normally be kept to a minimum.

V

Verbs – (see also 'auxiliary verbs', irregular verbs', 'modal verbs' and 'regular verbs') 'action' words, that change according to the tense used. Verb forms can be infinitive (see), past tense (saw), past participle (seen) or continuous (seeing).

CHAPTER 16: REFERENCE BOOKS

There are heaps of books on teaching English out there. Once you have the basics down, look for books with useful activities that you can picture your students doing. Other essentials include one chunky dictionary, a thesaurus and a grammar book.

Allen, V. F. (1983) Techniques in Teaching Vocabulary, OUP ISBN: 978-0194341301

Brown, Douglas, H. (2006) Principles of Language Learning and Teaching (Pearson) ISBN: 978-0131991286

Buttner, A. (2007) Activities, Games, and Assessment Strategies for the Foreign Language Classroom ISBN: 978-1596670648

Edge, J. (1993) Essentials of English Language Teaching ISBN: 978-0582025653

Griffith, S. (2003) Teaching English Abroad, Vacation Work Publications ISBN 1854582755

Harmer, J. (2007) The Practice of English Language Teaching, Longman ELT ISBN: 1405853115

Larsen-Freeman, D (2011) Techniques and Principles in Language Teaching, OUP ISBN: 978-0194423601

Leech, G (2001) An A-Z of English Grammar and Usage, Longman ISBN: 978-0582405745

Murphy, R (2004) English Grammar in Use, CUP ISBN: 0521532892

Swan, M. (2005) Practical English Usage, OUP ISBN: 0194420981

Widdowson, H.G (1990) Aspects of Language Teaching, OUP ISBN: 019437128X

White, R.V. (2001) The English Teacher's Handbook, Longman ISBN: 0952280817

Ur, P. (1996) A Course in Language Teaching: Practice and Theory, CUP ISBN: 0521449944

Ur, P. (2009) Grammar Practice Activities: A Practical Guide for Teachers, CUP ISBN: 0521732328

ABOUT THE AUTHOR

Mark Beales is an award-winning, best-selling author. After receiving a scholarship to study journalism, Mark worked as a reporter in England for 13 years.

In 2004 Mark moved to Thailand, where he began a new career in teaching. Mark has dragged his backpack to more than 40 countries, writing for Lonely Planet, Insight Guides and others. His work has also been published by CNN, The Guardian and The Bangkok Post.

Mark has worked in several international schools in Southeast Asia in various roles, including Head of Secondary, IB Diploma Coordinator and Head of English.

Mark has a National Professional Qualification for Headship (NPQH), a Master of Education (Distinction) and a Postgraduate Certificate of Education (PGCE) from the University of Nottingham, as well as a BA (Hons) in English Literature from Goldsmiths, University of London.

For more news about Mark's next books, visit markbeales.com.

Other titles by Mark Beales
Did You Know? Pointless trivia, killer questions & weird stories (2020)
Lonely Planet – Thailand 13th, 14th, 15th and 16th editions
Lonely Planet – The World's Best Brunches (2015)
Lonely Planet – The World's Best Spicy Food (2014)
Discover Thailand – 1st and 2nd editions
Lonely Planet: Project You – 1st edition
Lonely Planet: Southeast Asia on a Shoestring – 15th, 16th and 17th editions
Lonely Planet – Best in Travel (2011)
Lonely Planet: Cooks, Clowns and Cowboys – 1st edition
Insight Guides – Southeast Asia – 3rd edition

Insight Guides – Vietnam – Consultant / Author – 6th edition

Finally, if you did enjoy this book, we'd really appreciate it if you take time to leave a review. Many thanks.

THANKS

I am extremely grateful to all the students I have taught who have allowed me to develop as a teacher and understand exactly what they need. In addition I need to thank Mr Charles Soprano, a colleague and friend who was kind enough to lend his years of experience and proofread this text so expertly. Thanks also to my father for passing on his passion for English and education. Lastly, thanks to Ann, Daniel and Rey.

Printed in Great Britain
by Amazon